MANILA Manila and More

EDITED BY

Raymond Ang

WITH MANICA C. TIGLAO

AND MICHELLE V. AYUYAO

Made *of* Bricks

SERIOUS
STUDIO

Contents

Introduction

MANILA 1

MY POCKET
MaNiLa

Manila 2

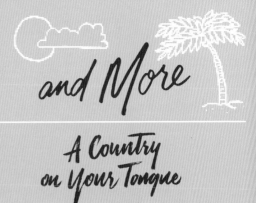

and More

It seems as if every problem, every crisis,
arises just to prove the aliveness of the city:
continually destroyed and continually rebuilt,
ever decaying and ever-re-greening.

MANILA

Manila

and More

When it was tagged "Pearl of the Orient"
in the '50s, Manila was known as Southeast
Asia's beautiful and progressive hidden gem.
Today, that moniker stands up for the city in
a different way: Getting to the heart of it
sometimes feels like prying a pearl from
a tightly-wound shell. But when Manila
reveals itself to you, it's unforgettable.

Introduction

I n Manila, no one hurries," *Harper's Bazaar* said in 1963, "the city has an aura that says—' enjoy your day'—and I should do just that. [...] The tropical beauty of the islands, the intensity of its night life and social whirl, the hospitality and gaiety of its people—all these combine to make a visit to the Philippines a delight." When the international fashion magazine wrote about Manila in 1963, the city was portrayed as a kind of tropical paradise, a must-visit for the American traveler on the lookout for the next big thing in travel.

Today, Manila is a city regarded as just something you pass through on the way to the Philippines's world-renowned beaches—at least that's what most international travel guides will tell you. One of the busiest and most urbanized places in the world, Metro Manila is composed of 16 cities and one municipality. It's dense and busy, tricky to navigate, and easy to get lost in. It's a far cry from the freewheeling tropical paradise *Bazaar* wrote about in 1963.

'The history of Manila can be put in three words: challenge and response,' Nick Joaquin wrote.

By the time the international fashion magazine wrote about the city in the early '60s, Manila had already gone through a few lifetimes.

Named after the nilad plant—a flowering mangrove plant that grew on the shores of the Manila Bay—Manila was the seat of the Spanish government when it gained sovereignty over the Philippine Islands in 1565, becoming the center of trade between Manila and Acapulco. Over 200 years later, in 1762, it was occupied by Great Britain for two years as part of the Seven Years' War. And in 1898, Manila was turned over by Spain to the United States in accordance with the Treaty of Paris, which effectively ended the Spanish-American War.

During World War II, most of Manila was destroyed, earning the grim distinction of becoming World War II's second most destroyed city after Warsaw, Poland. After the war, the City of Manila underwent "the Golden Age," and extensive revitalization efforts earned it the moniker "Pearl of the Orient."

"The history of Manila can be put in three words: challenge and response," the great Filipino writer Nick Joaquin wrote in his 1990 book, *Manila, My Manila*. "It almost seems as if every problem, every crisis, arises just to prove the aliveness of this city: continually destroyed and continually rebuilt, ever decaying and ever re-greening."

Getting to the heart of it sometimes feels like prying a pearl from a tightly-wound shell.

A few years ago, Manila was regarded as an up-and-coming Asian megacity, due to the influx of foreign investments, the buzz from the tourism industry, positive PR from talented Filipinos making it on the world stage, and an administration that seemed determined to stamp out corruption. Today, most of that sheen has rubbed off due to an increasingly controversial president and a political culture that seems to have gone back to old habits.

When it was tagged "Pearl of the Orient" in the '50s, Manila was known as Southeast Asia's beautiful and progressive hidden gem. Today, that moniker stands up for the city in a different way: Getting to the heart of it sometimes feels like prying a pearl from a tightly-wound shell.

Manila has always been politically volatile and while Manileños—and Filipinos—have been disappointed by one politician after another, some things never change: the people are unflailingly warm, the spirit is unswervingly tenacious, and Manila will always get back on its feet.

—RAYMOND ANG

Practical Checklist

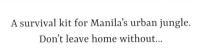

A survival kit for Manila's urban jungle.
Don't leave home without...

Cash

Not all establishments will accept credit cards. Treat cash as the norm, credit card service as an exception.

Foldable Umbrella

No matter the season, there's always a chance of rain. And in a city where public transport is a challenge, you'll thank yourself for keeping an umbrella handy.

Bottle of Water

Hydrate, hydrate, hydrate.

Sunblock

All that sightseeing will expose you to the harsh rays of the sun.

Sunglasses and Cap

Don't underestimate the sun. Protect yourself so you can have energy to see more.

Insect Repellent

Better safe than sorry.

Cultural Checklist

What you need to read, watch, and listen to before going to Manila

Read: *Ilustrado*
by Miguel Syjuco

(Farrar, Straus and Giroux, 2010)

The winner of the 2008 Man Asian Literary Prize, *Ilustrado* spans 150 years of Philippine history, alternating between a postmodern mystery, a political satire, and a meditation on identity.

Read: *The Woman Who Had Two Navels and Tales of the Tropical Gothic* by Nick Joaquin

(Penguin Classics, 2017)

Perhaps the country's most celebrated writer, the late great Nick Joaquin's body of work contemplates the questions and challenges of the Filipino people's new freedom after a long history of colonialism. In 2017, on the centennial of his birth, Penguin Classics compiled some of his best known short stories in this collection.

PENGUIN CLASSICS

NICK JOAQUIN
The Woman Who Had Two Navels and Tales of the Tropical Gothic
Foreword by GINA APOSTOL

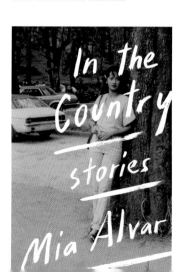

Read: *In the Country*
by Mia Alvar

(Vintage, 2015)

An award-winning collection of globe-trotting short stories that give voice to the experiences of the men and women of the Philippines and its diaspora, from fly-in models finding comfort in local urban legends to underemployed OFWs in the Middle East.

Watch: *Himala*
by Ishmael Bernal

(Experimental Cinema of the Philippines, 1982)

Very few films from the second Golden Age of Philippine Cinema are readily available on online services—thank God Ishmael Bernal's 1982 classic is on iTunes, then. Starring local film legend Nora Aunor, *Himala* is a film about the evils of blind faith—one that was brave in 1982 and still powerful in 2017. In 2008, *Himala* won the Viewer's Choice Award for the Best Film of All Time from the Asia-Pacific Region in the 2008 CNN Asia Pacific Screen Awards. In 2012, the restored *Himala* premiered at the 69th Venice International Film Festival.

Listen: *Here Lies Love*
by David Bryne and Fatboy Slim

(Todomundo/Nonesuch, 2010)

A concept album by the Talking Heads's David Bryne and the electronic artist Fatboy Slim, *Here Lies Love* tells the story of the rise and fall of former First Lady of the Philippines Imelda Marcos, the widow of the dictator Ferdinand Marcos, and the atrocities of the Marcos dictatorship. *Here Lies Love* features vocals from artists like Cyndi Lauper, Florence & the Machine's Florence Welch, Tori Amos, and St. Vincent.

Listen:
OPM Classics

The term "Original Pilipino Music"—more popularly known as OPM— gained popularity in the 1970s as a catch-all phrase for popular Philippine songs. Here's a primer on OPM—all available on Spotify, of course.

"Manila" by Hotdog
Perhaps the most iconic song of the '70s Manila Sound movement, seminal OPM band Hotdog's "Manila" has since become the unofficial anthem of the city. "I keep coming back to Manila," they sing. "Simply no place like Manila."

"Anak" by Freddie Aguilar
Folk singer Freddie Aguilar scored an international hit in the late '70s with this song, an ode to Filipino family values. Having been translated into 26 languages, it is possibly the best known OPM song around the world.

"I'd Give My Life For You"
by Lea Salonga
The Tony Award-winning singer and actress Lea Salonga is widely-regarded as a kind of national treasure. She originated the role of Kim in the musical *Miss Saigon* (where "I'd Give My Life For You" is from) at 18, became the first Asian woman to win a Tony, was the singing voice of Jasmine and Mulan in Disney's *Aladdin* and *Mulan*, and continues to act on Broadway and sell out venues like Carnegie Hall.

"Ang Huling El Bimbo" by Eraserheads
The winner of the 1997 MTV Video Music Award for International Viewer's Choice Award for Asia, "Ang Huling El Bimbo" is perhaps the very pinnacle of the OPM rock boom of the '90s. The legendary OPM rock band Eraserheads' signature song, "El Bimbo" has become a kind of hymn for many Filipinos.

"Tadhana" by Up Dharma Down
Up Dharma Down is an indie band that broke through in a big way in the 2010s. The last few years has seen "Tadhana" grow from a cult favorite to the theme song of a primetime TV series to the inspiration behind a blockbuster rom-com to one of the most covered songs in the country.

Frequently Asked Questions

How do I get there?

Manila is well-connected to the rest of the world. A lot of international airlines have direct flights.

When is the best time to visit the Philippines?

The best time is November to February, when it's neither too hot or raining too hard. During summer (March to May), temperature in Manila has been known to give heat strokes. And during rainy season (around June to August), your trip will be limited by the rain and the occasional typhoon.

What language do locals speak?

The Philippines is one of the world's largest English-speaking countries, with most of the population being able speakers of the language.

Filipino is the country's national language.

What's the best area to stay in?

This really depends on you but we suggest checking out the neighborhood guides in this book before booking. The book is structured according to neighborhoods because Manila is notorious for its traffic so to visit a neighborhood is to commit a few hours.

Is it enough to stay in Manila?

Yes and no. While the city has its hidden gems—this is what this book is about, after all—it would feel like a lost opportunity to go all the way to the Philippines and not see any of its beautiful sights.

What is the best way to get around?

Domestic flights are generally booked through the main local airlines Cebu Pacific, Air Asia, and Philippine Airlines, which serve the key provincial cities. Smaller players like Skyjet, Air Juan, and Air Swift are other options.

Within the city, the Manila Light Rail Transit System (LRT) and the Manila Metro Rail Transit System (MRT) both run through the city from north to south. Expect them to be crowded and unreliable though—Manila's transit systems have been known to break down every so often. A pricier alternative is, of course, to take a taxi or book a ride through apps like Uber and Grab.

For shorter treks, riding Manila's iconic jeepneys is definitely an experience.

How much do I tip?

There is no tipping standard in the Philippines. A tip of P50 is considered fair, but feel free to be more generous in the face of good service.

Where to Stay

PHOTOS BY JL JAVIER

A rriving in Manila can be a shock to the system. "Is the traffic always like this?" a tourist is bound to ask on the ride from the airport. The answer, more often that not, is yes—which is why the perfect accommodations are all the more important. In a city this congested, the hotel you pick is truly the neighborhood you pick. Thankfully, as varied and eclectic an experience as Manila is, the local hospitality industry has more than kept up. Here's a shortlist of accommodations for every type of traveler.

The Institution: The Peninsula Manila

Often referred to as the "grande dame" of Manila hospitality since its opening in 1976, the Peninsula is one of the most storied hotels in the city, and has maintained its genteel charm across over four decades of operations. It remains a favorite of upper-crust society not just for luxurious staycations but also for leisurely breakfasts at The Lobby, which frequently serves as a casual meeting spot for some of the city's most influential individuals. Particularly iconic for the magnificent *Sunburst* sculpture by National Artist Napoleon Abueva that adorns its vast ceiling, the Peninsula has become an institution in the city for the occasions that matter, including the New Year's Eve Ball that is an annual tradition for many families.

Cor. Ayala and Makati Ave., Makati
manila.peninsula.com
Price: $$$$

PHOTOS COURTESY OF THE HOTEL

The Luxe Pick: Shangri-La the Fort

Joining the Shangri-La Makati and the EDSA Shangri-La, the Shangri-La Group's third and newest venture in Manila houses the five-star Shangri-La Hotel and Residences, as well as the ultra-luxe Horizon Homes. The hotel offers 576 rooms and suites, and features seven specialty dining concepts, such as the Chinese fine dining restaurant Canton Road and premier steakhouse Raging Bull. Guests are also granted access to the exclusive Kerry Sports Manila, a members-only leisure and recreation club equipped with top-of-the-line fitness equipment and facilities, including an NBA-grade indoor basketball court and a multi-level children's playground.

30th St. cor. 5th Ave., Bonifacio Global City, Taguig
shangri-la.com/manila/shangrilaatthefort
Price: $$$$

The Entertainment Hotel: City of Dreams

The 6.2-hectare resort and casino complex offers one of the best gaming experiences to be had in the city, as well as topnotch entertainment thanks to its host of establishments, which includes superclubs Chaos Manila and Pangaea; an elevated version of the karaoke lounge, a popular pastime among locals; and the Shops at the Boulevard, lined with designer labels and upscale brands. Comprised of three luxury hotels, namely Crown Towers Manila, Nobu Hotel Manila, and Hyatt Hotel, City of Dreams offers an experience suited to every taste. Should one opt to stay elsewhere, the Manila outpost of Nobu, from world-renowned chef Nobu Matsuhisa, is a solid reason to visit.

Aseana Ave. cor. Macapagal Ave., Entertainment City, Roxas Boulevard, Parañaque
cityofdreamsmanila.com
Price: $$$-$$$$

The Time Travel: The Henry Hotel

Located in a compound that houses some 20 heritage homes in Pasay, the Henry Hotel is unlike most hotels run by international hospitality groups—and in this case, that's a good thing. You could be forgiven for thinking you've stepped back into another period—specifically the 1950s, when the compound was built—at this charming bed and breakfast nestled among five houses and decorated by multi-awarded designer Eric Paras. Featuring an Owner's Suite, regular suites, classic queen, and classic double guestrooms, the Henry Hotel is in good company, with furniture and design store A-11, Avellana Art Gallery, and the atelier of fashion designer Jojie Lloren all in the same compound.

2680 Compound, F.B. Harrison St., Pasay
thehenryhotel.com
Price: $$-$$$

The Boutique Hotel: Picasso Boutique Serviced Residences

Filled with nuances inspired by the artist from whom it takes its name, Picasso is one of the pioneers of the boutique concept in the city. Given that most of its guests are attracted to arts and culture, the creativity here begins with naming its rooms after the Spanish cities that influence their respective interiors—Malaga and Madrid, Barcelona and Montparnasse, Mallorca, and Andalusia. Apart from the usual amenities expected of a hotel, Picasso boasts an art gallery on the premises that regularly exhibits local contemporary art. Outside, the residential neighborhood is peppered with trendy cafés, chic eateries, and boutiques. Picasso is also within walking distance of the popular Salcedo Market held every Saturday, a must-visit for those residing in the area.

119 L.P. Leviste St., Salcedo Village, Makati
picassomakati.com
Price: $$-$$$

Serviced Residences: Aruga by Rockwell

After two decades of building posh residences, Rockwell Land has ventured into hospitality with Aruga Serviced Apartments. Aruga's well-appointed and fully furnished studio, one-, and two-bedroom suites are located across Power Plant Mall, and guests can request to be chauffeured around Rockwell Center via golf cart. A great option for those looking for anything from a one-night staycation to monthly or short-term rentals, Aruga's location within the Rockwell residential community makes for a pleasurable stay. Right outside its doorstep are an array of restaurants and salons. Guests may also access the membership-only Rockwell Club gym. For those who prefer a place further up north, Aruga has expanded to The Grove (117 E. Rodriquez Jr., Brgy. Ugong, C5, Pasig).

Waterfront Drive, Rockwell Center, Makati
arugabyrockwell.com
Price: $$$

PHOTO COURTESY OF THE HOTEL

PHOTOS COURTESY OF THE HOTEL

The Business Hotel: Makati Diamond Residences

One will be hard-pressed to find a reasonably priced hotel with a more ideal proximity to a variety of shopping and dining options, not to mention the Makati Central Business District. Perfect for travelers who place a premium on location, Makati Diamond is a no-nonsense hotel that offers a full range of amenities, from an indoor pool and gym, to a spa and TRX and yoga studios. When it's time to work, Makati Diamond Residences boasts of over 1,500 square meters of space available for business meetings. Its studios and one- to two-bedroom guestrooms are designed with a neutral color palette and outfitted with household necessities, ensuring utmost convenience for the business traveler.

118 Legazpi St., Legazpi Village, Makati | makatidiamond.com | Price: $$$

Hostel: Z Hostel

Situated in the heart of the thriving district of Poblacion in Makati, Z Hostel is mere steps away from a number of trendy restaurants and dive bars, and shopping centers like Power Plant Mall, A.Venue, and Century City Mall. Its own rooftop bar is an anchor of the neighborhood's nightlife scene, providing a fine skyline view and music. An affordable option for solo travelers, Z Hostel offers 128 beds in private rooms, an all-female dorm or the "stiletto room," and a mixed dorm for those looking for the complete backpacking experience. Each bunk bed is equipped with its own electric socket and reading lamp, as well as a locker where each guest can store gadgets and other valuable personal items safely. Keep in mind, however, that the hostel does not keep televisions in any of its rooms in an effort to encourage its guests to interact with each other—and the vibrant community beyond its walls.

5660 Don Pedro St., Poblacion, Makati
zhostel.com
Price: $

A Guide to
Local Cuisine

In the last few years, Filipino cuisine has become an emerging player in the international food scene. Whether it's our delicious ube landing on international trend-watching blogs or Filipino restaurants like New York's Maharlika and Washington D.C.'s Bad Saint making headlines in the *New York Times*, it seems like the time has finally come for our local cuisine to take center stage. Still, a lot of tourists will arrive in the Philippines with very little knowledge of the dishes that haven't yet been celebrated by international press. Filipino food isn't always pretty—presentation is not our strong suit. But if you can keep an open mind and a hungry stomach, you're bound for a few pleasant surprises.

Lechon

Lechon is a whole pig, removed of its innards, and stuffed commonly with lemongrass and garlic, then roasted on a spit. Once fully roasted, it is served with a side of sweet and tangy liver sauce. The lechon is commonly eaten on special occasions— fiestas, most of all—in the Philippines.

Adobo

Adobo is arguably the most popular Filipino dish—a sort of culinary ambassador to the world, the gateway dish to the rest of the cuisine. Some say the adobo—to *inadobo*, specifically—is more a process of cooking than it is an actual dish. Meat, seafood, or vegetables are marinated then left to simmer in a mix of soy sauce, vinegar, and garlic, resulting in dishes that are salty and sour, best eaten with rice and a side of tomatoes.

Dinuguan

Dinuguan, which quite literally translates to "stewed in blood," is a savory dish of pig offal cooked in thick pork's blood soup. Though intimidating at first, dinuguan is salty and tart, with bites of pork surfacing with each bite. It's paired with hot and buttery rice cakes called puto.

Kare-Kare

Kare-kare is a thick stew with a base of finely ground peanuts. Components of the dish include meat that may range from oxtail, pork trotters, tripe, and offal, alongside a selection of garden vegetables like eggplant, cabbage, green beans, and daikon. It is almost always served with a side of bagoong (shrimp paste) for added depth, and even a little heat for variants that are spiced.

Lumpia

Lumpia is the local term for egg rolls in the Philippines. Some may be fried, others served fresh. Stuffing varies as well, from pork or beef, to purely sautéed or fresh vegetables.

Nilaga

Nilaga is a classic and clean-tasting bone broth with beef or chicken mixed into the stock. Vegetables in the soup are potatoes, Chinese cabbage, and green beans, and some opt to include carrots and saba bananas into the mix as well. Patis (fish sauce) with a little calamansi are served on the side.

Paksiw

Paksiw is a cooking term that refers to seafood or meat simmered in vinegar, served on occasion with vegetables (dominantly for seafood). Oftentimes, leftover lechon is made into a paksiw that uses the lechon liver sauce mixed with vinegar.

Pancit

Pancit is the term used for noodle dishes across the board. It spans egg noodles, rice noodles, wonton, and even dry noodles, mixed in with sautéed vegetables, meat, and seafood, with different sauces. It's sometimes even mixed into soup.

Silog

A portmanteau of sinangag (garlic rice) and itlog (egg), the silog is a morning rice meal whose name varies with the main meat component it's served with. Tapsilog means tapa (marinated beef slices) with the rice, tocilog has tocino (sweetened pork), and longsilog has a side of longganisa (pork sausages).

Tinola

Tinola is a broth with a ginger base, using chicken as its main meat component. Veggies in the soup include long green peppers and young unripe papaya.

Sinigang

Sinigang is a sour broth made tangy traditionally with, though not limited to, tamarind. Souring agents for the soup, apart from tamarind, vary between calamansi, guava, unripe mangoes, and batwan. Beef, fish, pork, or shrimp are stewed in the broth with vegetables like tomatoes, radish, okra, and taro corms. Long green chillies are also included for optional spice, often crushed into a side of fish sauce with calamansi squeezed in.

Sisig

Sisig is made of chopped pork's face which has been boiled, grilled, then served on a hot plate. Chopped onions and chillies are mixed in, along with bone marrow and an egg on top, resulting in a pork dish that's equal parts crunchy, spicy, and creamy.

MANILA

PART 1

Manila can be chaotic and spiritual, dirty and divine, gritty and gorgeous all at once. If you don't find beauty and poetry here, you'll never find it anywhere

EDITED BY MANICA C. TIGLAO AND MICHELLE V. AYUYAO

MY POCKET

MaNiLa

BY CARLOS CELDRAN

I believe that Manila can be a reflection of your state of mind. Being a city of extreme contrasts, Manila can become an intense personal experience. It can be chaotic and spiritual, dirty and divine, gritty and gorgeous all at once. If you don't find beauty and poetry here, you will never find it anywhere.

Named after a white flowered mangrove plant and founded 327 years ago by the Basque conquistador Miguel Lopez de Legazpi, the gargantuan Metro Manila of today was once a little Muslim village ruled by a man named Rajah Sulayman.

IF YOU DON'T FIND BEAUTY AND POETRY HERE, YOU WILL NEVER FIND IT ANYWHERE.

Soon enough and not without friction, Rajah Sulayman's Malay Islamic system gave way to Spanish Conquistador Miguel Lopez de Legaspi's Christian rule in the year 1571. Then for the next 300 odd years, Manila, now known as Intramuros ("within the walls" in Latin) would stand as the seat of Spanish power in the archipelago.

Its grand government offices and soldiers controlled the state, while its priests and majestic cathedrals controlled the soul of the islands now called Filipinas (after Rey Felipe II). Its original wooden walls would be replaced by carved volcanic tuff as its bamboo huts and mosques would accede to seven baroque Catholic Churches surrounded by mansions made out of limestone, hardwood, and seashells.

MANILA IS A REFLECTION OF HOW DIFFERENT FLAVORS CAN MAKE UP A GREATER WHOLE, AND HOW TOO MUCH CAN SOMETIMES BE A VERY GOOD THING.

The city would grow in size and perception towards the end of Spanish rule. By the 19th century, the term Manila meant the surrounding districts outside the walled city as well, the extramuros (outside of the walls) to the original Intramuros. These areas included the Chinese immigrant district of Binondo, the retail quarter of Santa Cruz, the native intelligentsia and culturati borough of Quiapo, and the elite neighborhoods of San Miguel.

The advent of the American Colonial Period in the year 1898 would see extraordinary change in the city of Manila. In the year 1898, at a cost of 20 million dollars and the stroke of a pen upon a treaty from Paris, the Philippines would be suddenly passed on to the United States. Within the first decade of American occupation, Manila would reflect the influences of the new conqueror. Fresh from his success in designing Washington D.C. and Chicago, premier American city planner Daniel Burnham would revamp Manila's central core. Telephones, toothpaste, ice cream, and Coca-Cola would be introduced

to society and Intramuros's southern districts of Ermita, Malate, and Pasay would be converted from a row of seaside huts into a civilized collection of Art Deco and neo-classical structures, connected by wide roads and accentuated by parks and rotundas.

Then, just as quickly as the new structures and beliefs replaced the old ones, Manila would once again find itself in transition in the year 1945. But sadly, it would be a turn from which it would never recover. A victim of the battle between the United States Forces and the Japanese Imperial Army, the city of Manila would be brought to its knees through sword, and artillery. More than 120,000 lives would be lost, and only the San Agustin Church would remain standing in the original walled city of Intramuros. After the madness of war, the madness of reconstruction ensued. From the 1950's onwards, Manila grew at a radical rate. Greater Manila now includes the former provinces of Makati, Quezon City, Pasig, Parañaque, and Muntinlupa—their inclusion heralding the transition of the business and residential districts away from its original riverside core.

In the late 1960's, Manila would not only expand inland towards the Sierra Madre mountains but outwards and over the South China Sea as well. Snuggled right up to the city upon reclaimed land stands the Cultural Center of the Philippines complex, a development commissioned in 1969

by former first lady Imelda Marcos dedicated to the promotion of arts and international understanding. She would also commission the restoration of the walled city Intramuros in 1979.

I heard someone once say the jeepney is the perfect metaphor for the paradox that is Manila. Is it beautiful or is it grotesque? Is it inefficient or is it entrepreneurial? Is it just a common utility or is it a progressive work of art? Perhaps. But personally, I think that Manila is more like the halo-halo, that afternoon snack made out of a mind-boggling myriad of sweet beans, flan, shaved ice, and ice cream. Manila is a reflection of how different flavors can make up a greater whole, and how too much can sometimes be a very good thing.

Carlos Celdran is a cultural activist, a performing artist, and Manila's most famous tour guide. "There are tour guides, and there are tour guides. Should you visit the Philippines, see if you can still get Carlos Celdran," the New York Times says. For more on Carlos Celdran, *turn to page 103.*

NEIGHBORHOOD GUIDE:

QUEZON CITY

The true king of the North, this is the city where salt meets the earth and where gritty roads can lead you to the most unexpected of places.

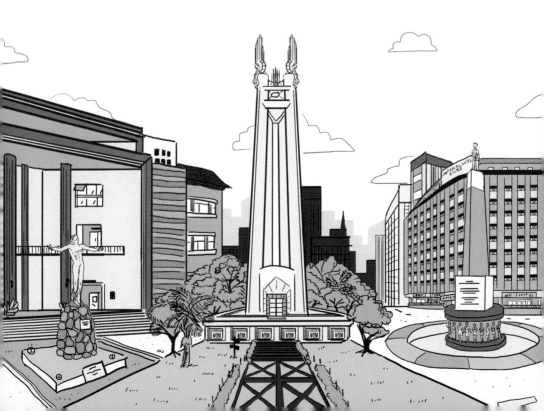

Quezon City, much like *Game of Thrones*'s Robb Stark, is the true king of the North—at least where Metro Manila is concerned. Named after former president Manuel Quezon, this was his "City of Dreams," a place slated to replace the city of Manila as the capital.

INSTITUTIONS

Here you will find the Office of the Vice President of the Philippines, known as the Quezon City Reception House (108 11th St., New Manila), as well as the home of the House of Representatives of the Philippines, known as the Batasang Pambansa Complex (Batasan Rd., Batasan Hills). Flanking these institutions are nearly every imaginable government office, catering to the almost three million residents of the city and beyond.

Two of the top colleges in the country can also be found in Quezon City. First is the main campus of the state university, the University of the Philippines (Diliman; upd.edu.ph), which also houses famous landmarks such as the Sunken Garden as well as

UNIVERSITY OF THE PHILIPPINES OBLATION

PHOTO BY JL JAVIER

the original Rodic's Diner where one can feast on shredded tapa and fried egg, and tour the extensive campus by way of a jeepney called the "Ikot." Second is the Ateneo de Manila University (Katipunan Ave.; ateneo.edu), which boasts the Ateneo Art Gallery (ateneoartgallery. org), the institution behind the Ateneo Art Awards, one of the country's most prestigious art prizes.

Also in the neighborhood is the contemporary art space Blanc Gallery (145 Katipunan Ave., St. Ignatius Village; blanc.ph), which hosts both emerging and established artists of various mediums. For lunch, the nearby Thai restaurant Basil (White Plains corner Katipunan Avenue; instagram.com/

basilphilippines) and the farm-to-table Earth Kitchen (Lot 10 B-10 Katipunan Avenue, earthkitchen.ph) are both worthwhile options.

If you're doing an art hop through Quezon City, West Gallery (48 West Ave.; westgallery.ph) cannot be missed. Run by artist Soler Santos, West Gallery is known for giving some of the biggest names in the local art scene their first breaks.

Minutes away from the two universities, past the many little restaurants along the foodie haven of Maginhawa Street in Teacher's Village, lie Tomas Morato and Timog Avenue. Their surrounding streets are

X FACTOR

Cubao X, once a haven for shoes, has been a revolving door of quirky, independently-run concept stores for over a decade.

3 General Romulo Ave., Cubao, Quezon City

Talas Manileño

The complex's dapper-maker—a nod to the classic old-timey barbershop, but with a few new tricks. Come in for a haircut with one of their courteous and skilled barbers; stay for a glass of scotch that pairs nicely with a delightful tête-à-tête and a scalp massage.

Kendo Creative

One of the latest in co-working spaces popping up all over the city—a haven for professionals for whom the office cubicle is not exactly pinned down. Their event calendar, which involves interesting workshops like crafting, coffee cupping, and cocktail making, is not to be missed.

Vinyl Dump Thrift Store

The home of the mythic sale rack with 10-peso records. Don't be fooled by its Thumbelina size; this place is wall to wall with great records. In fact, Vinyl Dump is so beloved among vinyl afficionados that it's where many of them meet every quarter to swap records.

Post Gallery

This is the funkier child of Pablo Gallery in Taguig—just as full of art, but with a more experimental nature and a curiosity for how art can be truly original. Swing by for their monthly Selecter FM spin sessions, which feature the work of select artists in various mediums.

THE CULTURE OF CONVENIENCE

The area of Maginhawa, which literally means "convenient," has become the go-to strip of treasure hunters on the prowl and gourmands looking for their next hole-in-the-wall adventure.

Pino does modern Filipino food that doesn't take itself too seriously, with dishes like kare-kareng bagnet (a peanut-based stew with deep fried crispy pork belly) and red wine adobong tadyang (short ribs cooked, adobo style, with a red wine base). Just upstairs is its sister restaurant, a vegetarian joint called Pipino. *39 Malingap St.; facebook.com/pinorestoph*

Yesteryears Music Gallery sells vinyl records, but the draw is the education that comes with each visit. Here you'll find records ranging as far back as the first Filipino recording artist, telling a tale of Philippine history by way of music. *44 Magiting St.*

Bookay-Ukay seems daunting with almost every inch of its space covered in books, but what seem to be carelessly strewn about are a good range of second-hand titles waiting for another bookshelf's love. *78 Maginhawa St.*

Shop Ilya In a predominantly Catholic country like the Philippines, sex shops are few and far between. In its colorful and whimsical brick-and-mortar location, Shop Ilya encourages sexual exploration with a tasteful selection of toys and other products. love. *189 Maginhawa St.; shopilya.com*

Van Gogh is Bipolar could play host to one of your most unusual and memorable dining experiences yet. The brainchild of Jetro Rafael, who manages his own bipolar disorder through cooking, Van Gogh is Bipolar's cuisine promises to be mood-altering and delicious. *154 Maginhawa St.*

Sweatshoppe Chilli Food Store will be of interest to the spice-inclined, who won't have to venture anywhere else with this store's extensive range of local and imported chili food items. *45 Malingap St.; facebook.com/sweatshoppe.tv*

Papa Diddis makes handcrafted ice creams in delectably unusual flavors. Anybody can scoop out a mound of chocolate, but how about some roasted forbidden rice, backyard farm tarragon, or coconut and lemongrass? *168 Maginhawa St.*

Mow's is the speakeasy of live music and spoken word, located in the basement of an unassuming Kowloon House. The setting is intimate and the acts fresh; a perfect way to cap off an evening along Maginhawa. *20 Matalino St.*

SWEATSHOPPE   PHOTO BY JL JAVIER

WITH THE CITY NOT ORIGINALLY PLANNED TO SUSTAIN MASSIVE STRUCTURES ITS BEST JEWELS LIE IN SMALLER SQUARE FOOTAGE.

SHOP ILYA   PHOTO BY SERIOUS STUDIO

commonly known as the "Scout Area," after the incredible loss of 20 boy scouts and their four scoutmasters in a deadly plane crash back in 1963. The Quezon City Council renamed 24 streets across six barangays after the boys in commemoration of their passing. These scouts never imagined that they would compose the hub of the local entertainment industry, as they host two of the biggest news and television networks in the country, ABS-CBN and GMA 7. The area, spilling over with local celebrities and working-class Filipinos with a penchant for song, is also characterized by its many karaoke haunts, like the famous Music Plaza 21 (27 Scout Tobias cor. Timog Ave.; music21plaza.ph).

After gaining a grasp on the major institutions that string together the heart of Quezon City, one will find that its populace is visibly composed of students, the working class, and their respective families. This is a city where, even in the advent of ride-sharing apps, the most common means of transportation still involve tricycles, jeepneys, and the Light Rail Transit (LRT). Similarly, while there are prestigious neighborhoods

afoot, this is not a city steeped in affluence or filled with skyscrapers. The University of the Philippines campus was constructed in the vein of the 1800s City Beautiful movement in America, which balanced urban structures with planned greenery to represent both harmony and order. This movement paved the way for areas like the Quezon Memorial Circle, and the presence of formal gardens around the city. Most homes that were initially constructed for mass housing were bungalows, which gave the city a rather flat look.

NIGHT LIFE

With the city not originally planned to sustain massive structures, its best jewels lie in smaller square footage. Route 196 (196-A Katipunan Ave.; facebook.com/Route196Rocks), a bar revered by fans of excellent live local music, is a compact and unassuming spot situated right by the gate to the suburban community of Blue Ridge. Likewise, Quezon City's definition of a night club doesn't possess the same flash one might see in Taguig

or Makati. Instead it has the snug but equally fabulous Today x Future (General Malvar St., Cubao; facebook. com/todayxfuture), where the dress code is broader than sparkly bondage dresses and five-inch stilettos, people spill over into the open street, and playlists range from ethnic chants to the best of Kylie Minogue. A more recent addition is 78-53-86 (White Plains West, 42 Katipunan Ave., White Plains; facebook. com/785386whiteplainswest), a minuscule bar that manages to do big things for its patrons by putting together a stunningly extensive vinyl collection—for play and not just display—with whiskey and cocktails.

What Quezon City offers to the weary soul is a stripped down, unfussy approach to exploring new tastes and new experiences, by way of its clearest strength: the discovery of intimate spaces. This is the city of casual dress and long lunches, of Sundays at lola's house and roving taho vendors saving your afternoon merienda. This is the city where salt meets the earth and where gritty roads can lead you to the most unexpected of places.

—GABBIE TATAD

DATE NIGHT

The bright lights, big dining of the Tomas Morato food strip might not seem conducive to quiet date nights. But in the corners of the area lie hidden gems with the kind of intimate ambiance conducive to getting to know your date better.

La Spezia

La Spezia boasts one of the city's most satisfying—and wallet-friendly—bisteccas. And the rest of the menu is similarly persuasive, boasting a solid selection of pastas and antipasto. 90 Sct. Dr. Lazcano St, Diliman; facebook.com/LaSpezia.MNL

Uno Restaurant

This humble bistro has been serving dependably good food in a quiet corner of Tomas Morato for over two decades now. Low key and intimate, it's not the easiest restaurant to find in the area but expect your persistence to be

rewarded accordingly. 195-C Tomas Morato Ave. cor.Scout Fuentebella, Laging Handa, Tomas Morato

Eighteen Bistro

So small it can only seat—you guessed it—18 people, Eighteen is the kind of dimly lit bistro you can imagine losing a few hours in, over wine and quiet conversation. Make sure to try the crowd favorites—chicken parmigiana and the spicy portobello and cream cheese pasta. Brgy. 1103, 51B Scout Rallos Ext., Diliman; facebook.com/pg/eighteenbistro

MARIKINA

Through the decades, the Shoe Capital of the Philippines has managed to retain its old rustic charm.

Once known as the Shoe Capital of the Philippines, Marikina has evolved into a dynamic city. Nestled among the wet markets and convenience stores are historical landmarks that date back to the Spanish era, adding to the charm of the quiet town.

Marikeños are typically early risers which explains the plethora of breakfast nooks and coffee shops. Among these is Rustic Mornings by Isabelo (11 Isabelo Mendoza St.; facebook.com/RusticMornings), a favorite dining place among breakfast lovers who like their servings big and their mugs overflowing.

RUSTIC MORNINGS

BY JL JAVIER

MARIKINA SHOE INDUSTRY

Just a stone's throw away from the restaurant is the Shoe Museum (J.P. Rizal St.; facebook.com/ ShoeMuseum) which houses some pieces from the 3,000-shoe collection of former first lady, Imelda Marcos. A few steps beyond it is the 200-year-old house of Don Laureano Guevarra (J.P. Rizal St., Sta. Elena; facebook.com/

cafekapitan), fondly referred to as Kapitan Moy, widely regarded as the founder of Marikina's shoe industry. Our Lady of the Abandoned Parish (V. Gomez St.; facebook.com/ OLAMarikinaOfficial), the city's oldest church, can also be found near the ancestral home.

RESTAURANTS

Marikina is best explored by foot, and some of its well-kept secrets are only discovered by doing so. Take, for example, Lilac Street, a long strip of hole-in-the-wall

restaurants that offer a variety of choices to suit any craving. Meat lovers will enjoy dining at Miguel & Maria (89 Lilac St., facebook.com/ miguelandmaria), while those who prefer desserts can try out Forget Me Not (24 Lilac St, facebook.com/ CafeForgetMeNot). Often frequented by millennials, the street is also home to a popular boutique, Empire Fashion Café (10 Lilac St.; facebook. com/empirefashioncafe), which houses several local fashion and makeup brands. A top choice among artists and writers is Greg and Sally Café (145 Ipil St., Marikina Heights; facebook.com/GregandSally), which is also conveniently located near the kitschy but one-of-a kind Book Museum (127 Dao St.; facebook.com/ BookMuseum). Cap the day off with a glass of wine at Fino Deli (151 Dao St., facebook.com/finodeli).

Marikina is the perfect in-between for those who like their history with a slice of cake and a cup of coffee. While slowly becoming a worthy destination for Manila's foodies, the old city's sense of nostalgia and love for good stories will keep anyone coming back for more.

—MICHI ANCHETA

RUSTIC MORNINGS

TRIUMPH LIKE A LOCAL:
Geraldine Roman

When Geraldine Roman won a congressional seat in 2016, she became the first transgender to ever be elected into the Philippines' House of Representatives. At the tail end of a particularly tempestuous election season, her historic victory became a beacon of light in a country that has always seemed "two steps forward, three steps back."

Since then, some of that Geraldine Roman magic has rubbed off. Navigating the constantly shifting political climate as a first-time congresswoman, some of Roman's moves have disappointed her most vocal supporters.

Still, that shouldn't overshadow what Roman's victory represents. In the only country in the world outside of the Holy See that still outlaws divorce, in a country that just a few years ago didn't have a Reproductive Health Bill, that win represents hope for the future, a promise of progress.

I know some people raise their eyebrows or talk behind my back, but I don't mind. I'll just do my work and do it well.

"I am living proof that, given the chance, people can lead normal lives and become productive members of our society, and be happy," she told *CNN Philippines Life* after winning the elections. "So why deprive them of this possibility, of this opportunity? Why be selfish?"

On prevailing discrimination against the LGBT community, she said: "My God, if they discriminate against women, can you imagine: What about transgender women? I know some people raise their eyebrows or talk behind my back, but I don't mind. I'll just do my work, and I'll do it well. And maybe by doing so, I can convince them that we're just ordinary people and we deserve respect. The same respect that you would want from other people."

WRITTEN BY RAYMOND ANG
PHOTOGRAPHED BY JOSEPH PASCUAL
SHOT ON LOCATION AT THE HOUSE OF REPRESENTATIVES, CONSTITUTION HILLS, QUEZON CITY

Can We Get a Better Deal This Time?

Philippine politics is difficult to understand for anyone visiting Manila—not to mention for its own citizens. In the face of a divisive and controversial administration, how do we negotiate Philippine politics?

By Nicole Curato

There are two quick and easy ways to make sense of Philippine politics: to affix our gaze to what is exotic, and to blame everything on culture.

An exotic view depicts the Philippines as a banana republic—a politically unstable country whose economy is driven by its single largest export: its own people. It elected for President a gun-toting firebrand who likened himself to Hitler for wanting to exterminate over three million drug addicts. Its municipalities are governed by warlords, the kind who runs their own private armies, massacres journalists, and amuses themselves with strange fetishes, such as crossbreeding a lion and a tiger in a private zoo. The Philippines' political class is dominated by dynasties and a few notable exceptions, including ex-military men, showbiz personalities, and the world's first and only eight-division boxing champion. Progressive politicians, it seems, can only dream of taking power from the nation's elite.

Why are things this way? Because, as the essentialist argument goes, the Philippines has a "damaged culture." People don't love their country. Filipinos have no discipline. They are stupid voters. The Philippines is so messed up that its citizens' ultimate dream is to change nationalities. Its celebrity-obsessed, patronage-driven political system is too stubborn to be reformed.

But as quick and easy explanations go, these depictions are both unfair and inaccurate. Instead of exoticizing and essentializing Philippine politics, taking a long and complex view leads one to realize that the nation's democracy is an outcome of a series of messy, vibrant, and sometimes triumphant negotiations.

Take the case of entrenched elite rule. The principalía that emerged during the Spanish colonial period maintained its power by striking a bargain with the American colonial authorities. The Americans left privileged local classes alone to accumulate wealth and run their towns like fiefdoms in exchange for access to resources, markets, and prime geographic spots to serve

The story of Philippine politics is also a story of people negotiating with power. The nation ousted a dictator in 1986. It stood up against the Roman Catholic Church and demanded the passage of the Reproductive Health law. Citizens took to social media to campaign against the misuse of pork barrel funds. **Politics is active in the public sphere.**

as military bases in the Asia Pacific. Unlike the case of post-war Japan, the historical juncture that could have redistributed political power was overridden by an elite bargain. The legacy of such bargain is felt until today.

But the nation's history is not only a product of elites negotiating with each other. The story of Philippine politics is also a story of people negotiating with power. The nation ousted a dictator in 1986. It stood up against the Roman Catholic Church and demanded the passage of the Reproductive Health law. Citizens took to social media to campaign against the misuse of pork barrel funds. Disaster survivors from Typhoon Haiyan mobilized in the streets to demand accountability and climate justice. Domestic workers in Hong Kong successfully organized to demand fair wages. The Philippines has one of the densest networks of civil society organizations in the world, suggesting that politics is not just limited to the state. Politics is active in the public sphere.

The negotiation of power continues to be ever more vibrant today, as citizens rethink what it means to be a democracy. Is democracy compatible with a strongman? Does death penalty have a place in a civilized society? Is shifting to a federal system of government the path to peace and prosperity, especially for the forgotten South? Should freedom of speech be restricted in the age of fake news?

The country's political future is being negotiated on these terms. Change is coming, Filipinos were told. One can hope that the public can get a better deal this time.

Nicole Curato is one of the country's most in-demand political commentators and a regular contributor to CNN Philippines. A sociologist by trade and discipline, she is a research fellow at the Centre for Deliberative Democracy and Global Governance at the University of Canberra.

NEIGHBORHOOD GUIDE:

SAN JUAN

Home to the second largest Filipino-Chinese community in Manila, the fast-changing San Juan has more to it than the traditional Chinese restaurants and delis one would have likely found a decade ago.

Walking through the exclusive enclaves of Greenhills, it can seem like not much has changed over the years in San Juan, home to perhaps the second-largest Filipino-Chinese community in Manila after Binondo (the original settlement of Chinese immigrants when they began relocating to the Philippines as early as 1954). The larger subdivisions here continue to be dominated by stately mansions occupied by affluent Filipino-Chinese families—but these days there are much more outside its gated communities than the traditional Chinese restaurants and delis one would have likely found a decade ago.

RETAIL AND LEISURE

The best way to get around is by car. Start with coffee at CO/OP (189 A. Mabini St.; facebook.com/ COOPmanila), a strikingly modern café and design store that stands out in its quaint environs. Head early to one of the city's shopping institutions, Greenhills Shopping Center (Ortigas Ave.; greenhills.com.ph), to browse for anything from export overrun clothing to local handicrafts and furniture. Constructed in the 1960s, the expanse, comprised of Unimart Supermarket, Shoppesville, and Virra Mall, became popular among San Juan youth. It remains a favorite of locals and tourists today, housing over 2,000 booths and stores that purvey nearly everything you can think of— even home décor, artworks, and stalls upon stalls of authentic South Sea pearl jewelry, which is a major draw at this shopping center.

Within the shopping center is an old culinary favorite of the Chinese-Filipino community, where the service is bare but the spare ribs a revelation, Le Ching Tea House (Shoppesville, Greenhills Shopping Center). Another culinary institution here is Gloria Maris (Missouri St., Greenhills Shopping Center; gloriamaris.com.ph), where families have convened for Sunday meals not for years but for generations. Nearby, more and more newcomers abound, like Carousel Creamery (8 Missouri St.; facebook.com/carouselcreamery), which isn't afraid to experiment with Filipino classics in its 101 ice cream flavors, introducing variants such as ube and pastillas, bacon and cheese, and even beer and chicharon.

After a long day of shopping, the Greenhills branch of The Spa (Promenade, Greenhills; thespa.com. ph) is a relaxing, luxurious option. If you're up for something different, the Chinese reflexology specialists at Foot Zone Day Spa (G/F, Richbelt Tower, 17 Annapolis St., Greenhills) have cultivated a loyal following and might provide an interesting experience.

GREENHILLS SHOPPING CENTER

ART AND CULTURE

For a dose of arts and culture, head to Cinema '76 Film Society (160 Luna Mencias St.; facebook.com/cinema76fs), a movie theater that champions independent cinema, for a chance to see local and foreign films outside the festival circuit; and Ronac Art Center (424 Ortigas Ave., North Greenhills), which has the contemporary art gallery Secret Fresh (facebook.com/secretfresh) as well as skate shop We Legendary (welegendary.com). Adding some cultural cachet to the neighborhood is Art Informal (277 Connecticut St., East Greenhills; artinformal.com), which has provided contemporary artists a platform to showcase their work since 2004. Meanwhile, the artist Juvenal Sansó, one of the country's most popular modernists, opened the Fundacion Sansó museum (32 V. Cruz St., San Juan) in 2014.

RESTAURANTS

While you're in Little Baguio, take the opportunity to sample the cozy neighborhood's dining options, which range from homey eateries beloved to residents such as Eat Fresh Hongkong Famous Street Food (J. Abad Santos cor.Biak na Bato St., Little Baguio) and Guevarra's (387 P. Guevarra St., San Juan), to delicious fare served in more modern interiors at Greeka Kouzina (285 P. Guevarra St., Little Baguio; facebook.com/GreekaKouzina), Oyasumi Ramen (308 P. Guevarra St., Little Baguio), and Tori Tori Kushiyaki Snack Bar (197 Wilson St.). Nearby, Pilates practitioners sweat out the calories at Onelife Studio Pilates (Citiplace Building, Jose Abad Santos corner Calderon St., Little Baguio; theonelifestudio.com). Thirsty Barber (G/F Promenade Building, Wilson St.; facebook.com/ThirstyBarberPH) seems like a bit of an anomaly in the area, but it is also the only place in San Juan you can get a haircut with a cocktail after.

There's no better place in this part of Manila to cap off a day than at EDSA Beverage Design Group (209 CLMC Building, EDSA, Greenhills-Mandaluyong; edsa-bdg.com), a cafe and bar that takes its craft beers, sodas, cocktails, and coffee seriously.

RONAC CENTER

BY JL JAVIER

MANDALUYONG

Its bevy of shopping malls makes it one of Metro Manila's centers for retail and leisure, but a stroll through its streets uncovers more than a few haunts that merit attention.

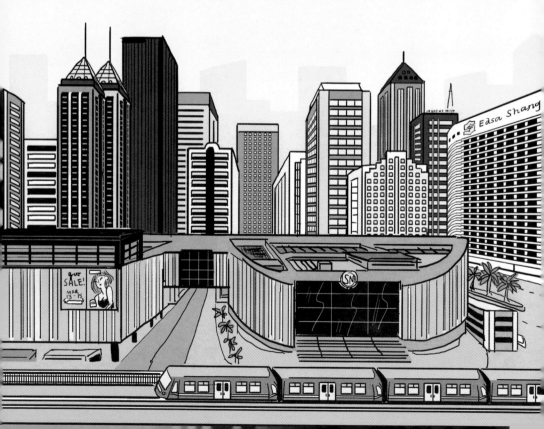

Closely interconnected with the cities of San Juan and Pasig, Mandaluyong is home to a number of schools as well as a greater part of the Ortigas business district. During the day it is populated by employees who work in the area, so it comes as no surprise that some of Manila's biggest malls are situated here as well. If we're being honest, a fair percentage of locals are inclined to spend most of their downtime in shopping centers, due in part to the cooler temperatures they offer as refuge from the tropical climate. Locals are thoroughly appreciative of any place where they can shop, see a movie, and dine—and the more options at which they can do all of the aforementioned, the better.

SHOPPING MALLS

SM Megamall (Ortigas Center; sm-megamall.com) is one of such supermalls, with some of the biggest local (among them Bench, Penshoppe, SM Department Store) and international (Crate and Barrel, H&M, Uniqlo, Zara) franchises' flagship boutiques alongside locally conceived brands like the café and music store Satchmi, the home extension of fashion label Aranáz Aranáz Tú, and the specialty eyewear boutique Ronnie & Joe. The mall's Fashion Hall boasts an impressive array of dining options on top of the great shopping— international names like Din Tai Fung and Tim Ho Wan rub shoulders with local institutions like Cibo and Abe and upstarts like Ooma and Bono Gelato.

Another major mall in the vicinity is Shangri-La Plaza (EDSA cor. Shaw Blvd.; shangrila-plaza.com), which houses some of the world's most recognizable luxury labels (Bottega Veneta, Jimmy Choo, and Saint Laurent can be found in the East Wing; the Homme et Femme boutique carries brands like Balenciaga, Marni, and Lanvin). For lunch, Green Pastures is often recommended for its delicious farm-to-table fare. Right across the mall, Chi, the Spa (EDSA Shangri-La Hotel, Ortigas Center, Mandaluyong; shangri-la.com) offers one of the most luxurious massages you'll find in Manila. Nearby, Climb Central (The Portal, Mayflower St., Greenfield District; climbcentral. ph) houses the country's largest wallclimbing facility and welcomes children and adults.

LIFESTYLE

To the west of the Ortigas area, about a 10-minute drive away, Mozaic Living (7 Sheridan St., Pioneer; mozaicliving.com.ph) once offered only Filipino-made

SM MEGAMALL

BY JL JAVIER

LOCALS ARE THOROUGHLY APPRECIATIVE OF ANY PLACE WHERE THEY CAN SHOP, SEE A MOVIE, AND DINE—AND THE MORE OPTIONS AT WHICH THEY CAN DO ALL OF THE AFOREMENTIONED, THE BETTER.

TACO VENGO

BY JL JAVIER

furniture, and while that was enough, it's to everyone's delight that they decided to turn a corner of their showroom into a café serving up coffee and some of the creamiest milkshakes in the city. A few minutes' walk farther down Pioneer is Sparta Philippines (126 Pioneer St.; sparta. ph), a sports and recreational training arena that offers martial arts, yoga, Zumba and crossfit, as well as an indoor soccer pitch for rent, and artbooks.ph (123 Pioneer St.; artbooks.

ph), an independent bookstore that carries rare art books and hard-to-find magazines with a concerted focus on Philippine art.

The beautifully designed Trader's Lounge (Philippine Stock Exchange Center, Exchange Rd., Ortigas), its name inspired by the financial hub in which it is housed, teems with young professionals in quest of craft coffee and libations day and night. The 24/7 Borough (The Podium, 18

ADB Ave., Ortigas Center; facebook. com/boroughph), a New York-inspired bar and restaurant, serves some well-loved pairings, like its grilled cheese and tomato soup, and milk and cookies, and hosts DJs a few times a week. Finally, Taco Vengo (16 Williams, Mandaluyong; instagram. com/tacovengo) serves some of the best tacos in the neighborhood along with a pretty strong drinks menu, making it one of the area's hippest evening spots.

Lifestyle 101

PHOTOS BY JL JAVIER

In the last few years, Manila's cultural scene has taken great strides. Suddenly, the city's arts and culture are thriving. A renewed interest in local contemporary art—bolstered by the stratospheric auction prices fetched by artists like Ronald Ventura—can be seen in increasingly anticipated annual events like Art Fair Philippines (February/March) and Art in the Park (April). The country's award-winning industrial designers are given a platform at the design and lifestyle trade fair Manila FAME (April/October). And the country's filmmakers—with directors like Brillante Mendoza and Lav Diaz now regular names at the world's major film festivals—are ushering in yet another golden age of Philippine cinema, in film festivals like Cinemalaya (July), Cinema One Originals (November), and even the more mainstream Metro Manila Film Festival (December). Of course, those annual events are not the only way to experience the best in Philippine culture. From independent shops and luxurious multi-brand boutiques to internationally competitive art galleries and age-old museums, these establishments continue to prove that Manila is more than its malls.

Ritual

"If you're in the Philippine capital and looking for original gifts for the folks back home, bypass the barong shops and head for Ritual," *Time* wrote in 2010. "This alternative grocery bursts with smart gift choices in the form of organic goods sourced from all over the archipelago." Long before the slow living movement found footing in Manila, Ritual proprietors Bea and Rob Crisostomo were firmly ahead of the pack, developing relationships with local farmers and finding ways to ensure that all their products were as conscientiously produced and ethically sourced as possible. They began by selling lemongrass deodorizer, laundry soap, and other organic items with old-fashioned labels at a weekend stall, before eventually opening a small store on the periphery of Manila's financial district. Today, Ritual continues to supply kitchen and lifestyle products free of chemicals and preservatives, and remains a platform for independent food entrepreneurs to sell their wares at an accessible location.

2/F Languages International Bldg., 926 Arnaiz Ave., San Lorenzo Village
ritual.ph

AC+632

At any given time of year, one can expect the window display at ac+632 to be elaborate and thoughtfully put together. It's almost impossible to walk past the store without doing a double take, as its windows are often a reflection of Ricky Toledo and Chito Vijandre, the colorful and fashionable pair who own the store. Filled with one-of-a-kind serveware, tabletop accessories, clothing, and other goods sourced in the Philippines and from various parts of the world, ac+632 also carries jewelry from celebrated Filipino designers such as Wynn Wynn Ong, Natalya Lagdameo, and the *Vogue*-featured Joyce Makitalo. It's unlikely you'll find any of the items on offer here at any other place in Manila—if you do, it will probably be at Firma, the other lifestyle boutique co-owned by the stylish duo.

2/F Greenbelt 5, Legazpi St., Ayala Center, Makati; facebook.com/AC632

Aranáz

Supporting local is a movement that is clearly afoot these days, but it certainly wasn't the case in the early millennium, when accessories designer and School of Fashion and Arts (SoFA) co-founder Amina Aranaz-Alunan established the Aranáz brand together with her mother Becky Aranaz and sister Rosanna Aranaz. Their brainchild is among a few Philippine labels that have successfully broken through the international scene in the last two decades, their exotic purses crafted with straw and other distinctly Filipino materials having earned editorial mileage in the likes of *Vogue*, *Harper's Bazaar*, and *Women's Wear Daily*. Today, with three boutiques in Manila, the label is helping redefine Filipino design, even giving rise to a spinoff brand in the home and design arena with Aranáz Tú.

Greenbelt 5, Makati; Rockwell Power Plant, Makati
aranaz.ph

Harlan + Holden

The fashion label has embraced the concept of uniform dressing, introducing beautifully tailored clothing pieces that are neither loud nor boring to the local retail landscape. Though its roots are proudly Filipino, Harlan + Holden eschews colorful tropical elements and native materials frequently associated with Philippine design, instead allowing three elements to define its aesthetic: neutral hues, roomy silhouettes, and light fabrics. Combined, they deliver easy, comfortable wardrobe staples designed to transcend numerous trends and seasons, wherever in the world they're placed.

SM Mega Fashion Hall, Mandaluyong; Greenbelt 5, Makati; Shangri-La Plaza, Mandaluyong; Ayala Malls the 30th, Pasig; Rockwell Power Plant, Makati harlanholden.com

Univers

Only three Filipinos have made it to the *Business of Fashion*'s prestigious 500 list, a definitive index of the people shaping the global fashion industry, and only one actually lives in the Philippines—Jappy Gonzalez, the man behind Univers. Manila has never been top of mind for designer shopping—in Asia, that distinction still belongs to cities like Hong Kong and Shanghai. But Univers—alongside its sister boutiques Homme et Femme and Archives d'Homme et Femme—is helping change that thanks to Gonzalez and his sweeping vision of what Manila retail is and what it can become in the not-so-distant future. Univers presents a lifestyle that embodies this. In this boutique, storied labels such as Céline and Balenciaga are on display alongside of-the-moment edits from Vetements and Public School; Maison Martin Margiela accessories sit across John Derian and Astier de Villatte plates, Cire Trudon fragrances, and even a home line by the celebrated Filipino chef Margarita Fores.

G/F One Rockwell, Rockwell Center, Makati hommeetfemme.ph

HARLAN & HOLDEN   PHOTO COURTESY OF BRAND

Kenneth Cobonpue

Schooled in industrial design at the Pratt
Institute in New York, Cebu-based Kenneth
Cobonpue has a long list of achievements
as one of the country's most prominent
designers who pioneered the revolutionary
use of rattan in furniture. Since breaking
through mainstream consciousness in
2010, when then Hollywood power couple
Brad Pitt and Angelina Jolie purchased his
designs for their home, Cobonpue has kept
a decidedly low profile, quietly earning
more awards (including Designer of the
Year at Maison et Objet Asia in 2014 and the
International Achievement in Visual Arts
from the National Commission for Culture
and the Arts in 2015) and finally establishing
his presence in Manila with a two-story
space that has on display some of the
designer's signature pieces alongside current
collections that are updated seasonally.

The Residences at Greenbelt, Esperanza
St., Legazpi Village, Makati
kennethcobonpue.com

a-11

At the Pasay showroom of interior designer Eric Paras, a winning play among textures, details, and styles extends to every surface. Prior to its opening in 2013, the venture was eagerly awaited by Paras's followers—and today it continues to be a sanctuary of sorts for the design-inclined, with its stock of curios and furniture by Paras and other designers here and abroad. Comprised of three houses erected in the 1950s, appointed by Paras, and stocked with his own designs alongside other designers', a-11 remains the best place to observe Paras' keen eye for detail while simultaneously sourcing eclectic souvenirs and objets d'art. Despite its diverse collection of homeware, contemporary and otherwise, it feels as if you've traveled back in time here, making a visit to a-11—and the creatively overhauled compound that surrounds it—all the more worthwhile.

2680 F.B. Harrison St., Pasay
artelano11.ph

Silverlens Galleries

The local art scene has evolved, and much of the credit belongs to the city's fearless visionaries, including the partners behind Silverlens, Isa Lorenzo and Rachel Rillo. The pair were at the forefront of transforming warehouses into gallery spaces when Silverlens opened in 2006. While several others have followed suit, Silverlens' courage in promoting photography as a legitimate medium of art in the Philippines and nurturing gifted young artists have reaped their rewards. If you're looking to uncover the next big thing in local contemporary art today, you've come to the right place—the gallery has earned a reputation for identifying true talent after nurturing a roster of artists who have swiftly gained international recognition, among them Maria Taniguchi (Hugo Boss Asia Art 2015), Martha Atienza (Baloise Art Prize at Art Basel 2017), and Pio Abad (Dazed and Confused Emerging Artist Awards). The gallery's new home continues to host exhibitions that are always exciting and insightful, and with a distinct curatorial identity that is helping define Philippine contemporary art as we know it.

2263 Chino Roces Ave. Ext., Makati
silverlensgalleries.com

The Drawing Room

An essential stop on any worthwhile Manila art crawl, The Drawing Room is one of the most influential galleries in town. Established by Cesar Villalon Jr. in 1998 as a specialist venue for works on paper, it has progressed dramatically throughout the years, lodging works of varying mediums and platforms. Though the gallery moves with ease from exhibiting drawings and paintings to mounting ambitious large-scale installations, this is not always the place to discover emerging talent, as majority of its represented artists are boldfaced names in the world of art—Mark Justiniani, Mark Salvatus, and Alfredo and Isabel Aquilizan, to name just a few, who mutually benefit from The Drawing Room's strong international presence by way of partnered exhibits with other galleries in London, Singapore, Beijing, Taipei, Turin, and Jakarta and participation in prestigious art fairs such as the Scope Art Fair in New York, Art Stage Singapore and Jakarta, Asia Now Parisian Art Fair, and Art Basel.

Karrivin Plaza, 2316 Chino Roces Ave. Ext., Makati
drawingroomgallery.com

THE DRAWING ROOM

Metropolitan Museum

Enclosed within this stately institution's walls is a behemoth collection of Philippine art spanning centuries, historical periods, and artistic movements. Originally conceived in 1976 as a local venue for traveling international exhibitions, the Metropolitan Museum has since adapted its vision in order to showcase the rich history of the country's cultural fabric. Much of the works on display belong to the Bangko Sentral ng Pilipinas, including the permanent collections that detail the evolution of Philippine heritage, with religious art, 8th- to 13th-century classical pottery and goldwork from the pre-colonial period, and a landmark exhibition featuring contemporary art from both the Philippines and abroad. To visit the Met is to take the first step in tracing the trajectory of Philippine art from the past, to the present, and to where it's headed.

Roxas Boulevard, Malate, Manila
metmuseum.ph

Museum of Contemporary Art and Design (MCAD)

Housed within the De La Salle-College of Saint Benilde's School of Design and Arts, the contemporary art museum's curatorial direction is largely in line with the programs offered by the educational institution, which range from fashion design, film, and multimedia, to architecture, music production, and animation. The goal of the space is not merely to serve as a platform for the artists in training here, but to challenge creativity and further artistic growth among and beyond the student population by hosting both local and international exhibitions. One of the more recent additions to Manila's museum scene, MCAD has welcomed a slew of shows by significant local and international artists.

De La Salle-College of St. Benilde School of Design and Arts, Dominga St., Malate, Manila
mcadmanila.org.ph

METROPOLITAN MUSEUM

GREENHILLS SHOPPING CENTER   PHOTO BY JOSEPH PASCUAL

Greenhills Shopping Center

Whether you're looking to shop or just survey what the local scene has to offer, a visit to Manila isn't complete without a quick trip to the city's most popular bazaars. Peddling a wide variety of items—from export overrun clothing and secondhand designer goods to Philippine handicrafts and authentic South Sea pearls that have lured the likes of singer Rihanna and even Queen Sofia of Spain to this side of town—this bazaar's offerings run the gamut from bargains to high-quality finds. Located on 16 hectares of land, the sprawling complex has undergone a number of renovations since its establishment in the early 1970s, welcoming a slew of new buildings housing bigger and more modern stores in addition to its famous shopping stalls throughout the years, but it has remained a favorite shopping destination for generations of families.

Ortigas Ave., Greenhills, San Juan
greenhills.com.ph

National Museum of Natural History

Housed in the former Department of Tourism building, the National Museum of Natural History showcases the Philippines' flora and fauna. The museum itself is a work of art. While the interiors remain faithful to the neo-classical style of the original 1939 building, architect Dominic Galicia's design features a double-helix DNA-inspired structure—the building blocks of life—called the "Tree of Life" that towers over a central courtyard.

"It distills into one symbol mankind's primordial quest to understand his environment, a quest that was perhaps sparked by man's first of curiosity," Galicia's firm says on their website. The newly renovated National Museum of Natural History-opening in 2018-completes the triumvirate of museums run by the National Museum of the Philippines, which includes the National Museum of Fine Arts (formerly called the National Gallery of Art) and the National Museum of Anthropology (formerly the Museum of the Filipino People).

Ermita, Manila
nationalmuseum.gov.ph

NATIONAL MUSEUM OF NATURAL HISTORY
PHOTO COURTESY OF DOMINIC GALICIA ARCHITECTS

TRIUMPH LIKE A LOCAL:
Pia Wurtzbach

It took Pia Wurtzbach three tries before she became the third Filipina to be crowned Miss Universe in 2015. Which seems apt—after all, what could be more Filipino than tenacity?

"Once you [live in] Manila, you can pretty much survive everywhere else," she says. "Because you learn how to be street smart—that's not something you learn in school. When you're out there and hustling in Manila, you can make it everywhere else."

Before finally taking home the crown, Wurtzbach had already joined Binibining Pilipinas—the pageant that finds the country's representative to Miss Universe—twice, winning 1st Runner Up in 2013 and only placing in the top 15 a year later. And even in victory, a now-famous mistake by host Steve Harvey threatened to steal the thunder of her Miss Universe triumph, when he mistakenly announced her as the runner-up instead of the winner. But true to form, Pia Wurtzbach took it all in stride.

Whether it's home or not, Manila feels like home.

She's been reaping the rewards of that tenacity ever since. As Miss Universe, Wurtzbach has traveled the world, fulfilling her duties to the crown and representing the Philippines on the world stage. Still, after seeing the world, Wurtzbach says there's no place like home. "Whether it's your home of not, Manila feels like home," she says. "Whether you live here or not, you adjust to it quite fast."

"It's not too harsh, living in Manila. I mean, yes, it's really humid and life is tough in the Philippines. But when you're really up for it, and you really want to experience it, you'll find that you fall in love with it really quickly. I would say it's the people, definitely. We make it so fun."

WRITTEN BY RAYMOND ANG
PHOTOGRAPHED BY BJ PASCUAL FOR TEAM MAGAZINE
SHOT ON LOCATION AT STUDIO BJ PASCUAL, MAKATI CITY

24 Hours with Miss Universe

Five things every tourist has to do in Manila, according to Pia Wurtzbach

1. Retail Therapy
"Don't we love our malls? I'll have to take them to one of our big malls, just to show them how much we love our big air-conditioned malls and how people just [hang out] there."

2. Ride in Style
"Involuntarily, they'll realize that Manila traffic is crazy. I'll make them ride a jeepney! If they're game, *sabit* (to ride hanging from the back of the jeepney). If not, they can sit inside."

3. Eat Through the City
"There will be a lot of food involved. I would make them try street food in the University of the Philippines—I think that's nice because it feels like a college town. There will definitely be halo-halo—the classic version with ube ice cream. I love explaining it to them. 'Halo-halo actually means 'mix-mix.' In the Philippines, we love to say things over and over.' [Laughs]"

4. Night Moves
"I will show them the nightlife also. If they're up for it, we'll go karaoke. If not, we'll go to one of the big clubs. Definitely we have a great nightlife. Sometimes when I'm abroad, I can't help but compare our nightlife to theirs. I think, 'Ah, it's more fun in the Philippines.'"

5. History Lesson
"We should also do [a tour of] Intramuros. They see a bit of history there. If there's time, we'll ride kalesas (horse-drawn carriages)."

PASIG

Often overlooked in favor of bigger cities like Makati and Taguig, the quieter, quainter Pasig has nonetheless made itself known as one of Metro Manila's food capitals.

Quieter, quainter, and often overlooked in favor of bigger cities such as Makati and Taguig, Pasig has welcomed an ever-growing number of visitors in recent years, having become synonymous with food. But to come here solely for a restaurant crawl, as most have done in the past, would be a mistake, as there is much to be explored in Pasig apart from the longtime favorite eateries and hole-in-the-wall diners responsible for the buzz around the neighborhood of Kapitolyo.

LIFESTYLE

While the Lopez Museum and Library (Benpres Building, Exchange Road, San Antonio, Pasig; lopez-museum.

com) is slated to relocate to a newer and larger space in Rockwell, for now it remains at its original home, a heritage building constructed in 1969. The edifice had been envisioned by media tycoon Eugenio Lopez Sr. as the headquarters of his *Manila Chronicle* newspaper, which would shutter at former president Ferdinand Marcos's declaration of Martial Law.

Also in the area is the larger second branch of Felipe and Sons Barberdashery (El Pueblo Real de Manila, J. Vargas Ave. cor. ADB Ave.; felipeandsons.com), where one can get a haircut, a bespoke shirt, and a drink all in one go. For all things interiors, head to CW Home Depot Ortigas (Julia Vargas Ave.) for variety and range, and Space Encounters (Padilla Building, F. Ortigas Jr. Road, Ortigas Center; spaceencounters.net) for mid-century modern furniture. Though Kapitolyo's narrow streets

offer plenty of gems, nearby there is also what is perhaps the biggest commercial complex in the area, the recently developed Capitol Commons, which adds a variety of shopping and dining options, including a café version of New York's Filipino cuisine institution Purple Yam. A few minutes away is Philsports Arena (Philippine Sports Complex, Capt. Henry Javier St.), known simply as Ultra, where you might spot a celebrity or two jogging their way through the track oval. If you're in search of an adrenaline rush, there is also the Ninja Academy (Dr. Sixto Antonio Ave.) for parkour, or Jump Yard (Frontera Verde Complex, Ortigas Ave. cor. C-5), a trampoline park gaining traction among the young—and the young at heart.

Meanwhile, Ayala Malls the 30th offers an intimate line-up of quality homegrown and international establishments, from Churreria La

PASIG HAS WELCOMED AN EVER-GROWING NUMBER OF VISITORS IN RECENT YEARS, HAVING BECOME SYNONYMOUS WITH FOOD.

Maripili to Boston ice cream parlor chain Emack & Bolio's.

RESTAURANTS

Kapitolyo might be the word on the street for food, but there are certainly other spots for a stellar meal to be had. Minami Saki (Astoria Plaza, Escriva Dr., San Antonio Village) offers excellent modern Japanese cuisine, as does Marufuku (Crescent Building, 29 San Miguel Ave., Ortigas). City Golf Plaza is another burgeoning food destination and Lo de Alberto (City Golf Plaza, Ugong), a taqueria specializing authentic and straightforward Mexican cuisine, is one of its most promising tenants.

LOCAVORE   PHOTOS BY KAI HUANG

SERIOUS EATS

Where to go for the best meals in the food neighborhood Kapitolyo.

Café Juanita

An old favorite for its sophisticated but unintimidating take on Filipino cuisine. *19 West Capitol Dr.; cafejuanita.com*

Charlie's Grind & Grill

This no-nonsense joint has earned a cult following for its quality wagyu and angus burgers at reasonable prices. *16 East Capitol Dr.; facebook.com/charliesgrindandgrill*

Poco Deli

This neighborhood haunt is beloved for its chocolate cake, extensive range of sausages, and beers and wine. *21 East Capitol Dr.; pocodeli.ph*

Silantro Fil-Mex Cantina

This spot doesn't claim authenticity, embracing the Filipino influence on its nachos, burritos, quesadillas, and more. *75 East Capitol Dr.; facebook.com/silantrofilipinomexicancantina*

The Good Seed

Tasty fare that's vegan- and vegetarian-friendly. *3 Brixton St.; edgyveggy.ph*

Three Sisters

Famous for its heirloom Filipino recipes, the eatery is known for its pancit and barbecue. *136 West Capitol Dr.; threesistersrestaurant.com*

There Goes the Gayborhood

BY PAOLO LORENZANA

While it remains very much a Catholic country—one where separation of church and state is largely fictitious—the Philippines might surprise you on how LGBTQ-friendly it is. A few years ago, a global survey found that the Philippines is one of the most gay-friendly countries in the world, citing the relatively high level of public acceptance for the community. And while there's still a lot of room for growth and education in the conservative and largely traditional country, it's not a bad start. Paolo Lorenzana, the editor of *Team*, the only gay magazine in the country, shares his picks for a night out in the gayborhood.

Cuore Bistro & Social Lounge

One of the few—if not only—restaurants in the city with a rainbow flag up front. Also known for their Spotlight parties, where your glow stick illuminates your romantic status (rainbow if you're LGBT). Valdelcon Building, 20 Jupiter St., Makati; instagram. com/cuoremnl

Pineapple Lab

A safe exhibition space for art, no matter how fruity it can get, from the boy-on-boy shibari demonstrations of 2016's Kink Karnival, to boylesque performed to Beyoncé at their Gayborhood nights.
6071 R. Palma St., Makati; pineapplelab.ph

O-Bar Lab

World-class queens perform like divas at the Superbowl halftime. Sunday nights serve up the best show in the city, enough to distract you from that guy shooting glances from the bar.
Ortigas Home Depot, Julia Vargas Ave., Ortigas, Pasig; instagram.com/obarphilippines

Rapture-Klubdude

A cruise-y, ratchet escape for unpretentious gays. Grab the mic for videoke or be prepared to let someone grab you on the dance floor.
G/F R&F Bldg., 903 Aurora Blvd., Cubao, Quezon City

Nectar Nightclub

The first out and proud LGBTQ club in Bonifacio Global City, the center of Manila nightlife, Nectar is the brainchild of the forces behind the all-demographics popular Valkyrie Night Club and the classic Malate gay bar Bed. Sashay in for Poison Wednesdays, where anyone from femmes, fats, or fag hags can feel welcome. Discrimination dies from the venom of anything-goes DJ sets and an anything-goes crowd. Order the Poisonous Nectar with "coconut cum."
The Fort Strip, 5th Ave., Bonifacio Global City, Taguig; instagram.com/nectarofmanila

STRIPED SHIRT, JOSEPH; NECKLACE, CURA V.

SHOP LIKE A LOCAL:
Liz Uy

There was a time Liz Uy was primarily known for her thoroughly glamorous life, the striking fashion editor of *Preview*, the country's biggest fashion magazine, who had managed to capture the hearts of some of the country's most famous bachelors—John Lloyd Cruz, the country's favorite leading man, and Noynoy Aquino, the 15th president of the Philippines. But anyone who thought Liz Uy could be defined by the men she stood beside would be proven wrong.

Right under the public's nose, Uy was turning herself into a true fashion force, graduating from editorial life to become the country's biggest stylist—helping mold the personas of the country's biggest stars—and a bestselling author (*Stylized: Liz Uy's Ten Style Essentials*), helping mold the aesthetic of a whole country.

As her international profile has grown, Uy has made it a point to use her platform to support the local fashion industry.

In the last few years, Liz Uy has steadily grown her fashion empire, evolving into an increasingly international fashion star in front of Filipinos' eyes. Her street style has become a staple in the world's fashion authorities, turning the heads of everyone from Net-a-Porter to the *New York Times*'s late great street style maverick Bill Cunningham. And Uy herself—having signed with modeling agency The Society Management, the same company that represents Kendall Jenner—has been featured by both of-the-moment digital destinations like *The Coveteur*, as well as the preeminent fashion bible *Vogue*. As her international profile has grown, Uy has made it a point to use her platform to support the local fashion industry.

In her street style snaps in fashion publications like *Bazaar*, for example, you'll see her pair an of-the-moment Balenciaga or Gucci statement piece with reliable staples by Filipino designers like menswear savant Joey Samson or the young Carl Jan Cruz. When she took over the Instagram account of travel authority *Condé Nast Traveler* (a global audience of more than 1.8 million followers), her posts were characterized by majestic views of the beaches of Palawan as well as strategically placed beach-ready pieces by local brands like Aranáz.

Luxuriating among the locally made products in Lanai, the lifestyle boutique she picked as the location for this shoot, Uy says, "Our designers are passionate, hardworking, driven, and adept at producing garments with impeccable tailoring and craftsmanship. It is endearing how they can work in these sort of old-school ways and produce of-the-moment pieces... They are able to effectively bring a combination of creativity and a spirit of our culture into their designs. On a global scale, that's what it's all about nowadays."

WRITTEN BY RAYMOND ANG
PHOTOGRAPHED BY BJ PASCUAL
MAKEUP BY LALA FLORES / HAIR BY RAYMOND SANTIAGO
SHOT ON LOCATION AT LANAI, THE ALLEY AT KARRIVIN PLAZA,
2136 CHINO ROCES EXT., MAKATI

The Stylist's Picks

Liz Uy's go-to local designers

Bags
Rita Nazareno of Zacarias 1925 (zacarias1925.com)
Malou Romero of Joanique (joanique.com)
Amina Aranaz of Aranáz (aranaz.ph)

Jewelry and Decos
Ann Ong (annongjewelry.com)

Denim
Carl Jan Cruz (carljancruz.com)

Hats and Head Pieces
Mich Dulce (michdulce.com)

ESSENTIAL MEALS

In the past few years, Manila's dining scene has taken great strides thanks to a burgeoning economy and a generation of young chefs reinventing Filipino food. From farm-to-table by Asia's Best Female Chef to market buys near Manila's harbor, here are nine of Manila's most in-demand tables.

PHOTOS BY GABBY CANTEROS

Grace Park

One cannot talk about the Philippine dining scene without mentioning the force that is Margarita Forés, who in 2016, was named Asia's Best Female Chef by The World's 50 Best Restaurants list. Responsible for introducing accessible Italian dining in the country through her popular restaurant chain Cibo, Forés has since come to champion the local farm-to-table movement.

Her continuous work with farmers around the country has birthed a newfound appreciation for locally grown produce, which is manifested in her menu for Grace Park. The place looks like a provincial cottage, with ceilings left unfinished and cutlery intentionally mismatched, providing a fitting backdrop to the bucolic nature of her food. Her expertise in Italian cooking still echoes through Grace Park, notably making use of

ingredients from all over the country: mezzi rigatoni with lemon confit and crab fat from Alaminos, burrata made in Negros with red wine tomatoes, organic Batangas duck breast with some Mindoro rambutan. Grace Park's menu changes regularly, depending on what comes in fresh from the farms.

The restaurant is also known for its initiatives to learn more about the country's varied native dishes, through its Regional Cuisine Series. Home cooks from different regions in the Philippines are invited to share their expertise on the cuisine of their province, through a special menu in Grace Park.

G/F One Rockwell Building, Rockwell, Makati
+63917 513 8945 / +632 843 7275
margaritafores.com

GALLERY VASK

Gallery Vask

Leading the kitchen of Gallery Vask is Spanish native Luis Gonzalez, who found his way to Philippine shores in search of adventure. A former club owner and DJ, Gonzalez traded in clubbing for cooking, and hustled in various Michelin-starred restaurants around Spain, including the restaurant group behind Mugaritz. He then traveled to Manila where he started from zero.

What blossomed from Gonzalez's mind became a culmination of his exposure to modern Spanish cooking, and ingredients discovered through his travels around the country. Components of the degustacion-only menu may vary from an ingredient indigenous to a particular province—like a crisp and freshly plucked leaf from Pampanga, which tastes almost exactly like the tart peel of a sour apple—or an existing dish characteristic of local cuisine.

Gonzalez's ingenuity has attracted international attention, and has earned Gallery Vask the 39th spot on Asia's 50 Best Restaurants for 2016, making it only the second restaurant from the Philippines to be included. In 2017, it climbed four spots to number 35. Vask has proven that it doesn't just further the Philippines's culinary presence on the global stage, it also gives its diners a newfound appreciation for the country's bounty.

5/F CLIPP Center, 39th St., Bonifacio Global City, Taguig
+63917 546 1673; vaskmanila.com.ph

Mecha Uma

Mecha Uma is a collaboration between Bruce Ricketts, one of the Manila restaurant scene's poster boys, and The Moment Group, the country's fastest growing restaurant group. Its name is a portmanteau of the Kansai words *mechakucha* (absurd) and *umai* (delicious), resulting in a menu of foolishly tasty dishes.

To be clear, Mecha Uma is not a Japanese restaurant. Rather, it takes its cues from various global cuisines, and incorporates the pulse of Japanese taste in its dishes. Ricketts is notorious for his repertoire of ingredients, like the sparkling firefly squid, and sought-after cod sperm.

In 2016, The Diners Club included Mecha Uma on their 50 Best Discovery Series, a prestigious list of the next generation of dining destinations around the world.

1/F RCBC Savings Bank Corporate Center, 25th St., Bonifacio Global City, Taguig
+632 801 2770
mechauma.ph

Your Local

Your Local's logo has its "A" discreetly flipped over. You won't notice it at first glance, but it's there—the hint that this restaurant has surprises up its sleeve. Your Local has stamped itself as the city's go-to for Pan-Asian food updated to suit the taste of the times. In Your Local, laksa might take the form of fettuccine, while fried rice might earn bits of Korean spiced wagyu.

Since setting the course for offbeat oriental entrées, Your Local's brightest stars are its beef rendang buns and torched salmon donburi. The first takes fried mantou buns and stuffs them with a fiery beef rendang, smoked aioli, and pickled cucumbers. The latter is a rice bowl brimming with textures and flavors, as a mix of red rice and corn kernels mark the base for torched salmon with a creamy head of mentaiko and leeks.

Your Local's innovations have given Manila's dining scene a breath of fresh air, so much so that they've been recognized internationally, with mentions in *Bon Appétit* (for the salmon donburi) and *Condé Nast Traveler.*

106 Esteban St., Legazpi Village, Makati
+632 823 6206
yourlocal.ph

Seaside Dampa

A highly underrated Manila dining destination is the Seaside Dampa, just a few minutes away from Manila's harbor. A satellite fish market, rows of stalls boast the latest catch from provincial waters. There's an assortment of fish, shellfish, and seaweed, all of which can either be bought to be taken home or cooked right there. This is how it works: diners make their rounds and purchase the seafood, then take them to any of the nearby restaurants called palutuan (quite literally, a place to get things cooked). Here, menus list the ways in which main ingredients can be cooked, and are priced according to the weight they come in. Meals here are simple yet tasty, and surprisingly cheap for the amount of food you get.

Though often overshadowed by the city's increasingly exciting dining scene, Dampa has the potential to be, for Manila, what hawker centers are to Singapore.

Macapagal Boulevard, Pasay

Toyo Eatery

Not much on Toyo Eatery's menu is traditional Filipino cuisine, but this restaurant might be the city's best case for the cuisine's potential global conquest. Headed by Jordy Navarra, Toyo Eatery heightens and hones familiar local flavors, and turns them into something more refined.

A Toyo staple, for instance, is inspired by the popular Filipino barbecue, a street food comprised of pork meat on wooden sticks cooked on coal grills by the streets. Toyo's three-cut pork barbeque is a medley of pork belly, leg, and shoulder, threaded through a bamboo stick, charred, then glazed. Something as basic as the bread basket at the start of the meal is an opportunity to pay tribute to Filipino breakfast—bread rolls are a cross between the traditional morning pandesal bread and the buttery pastry ensaymada, with fragments of rosy breakfast staple tocino peeking out between each fold.

Navarra's chef-d'oeuvre, however, is the garden salad, inspired by the popular Filipino folk song "Bahay Kubo." The song—which lists the vegetables indigenous to the Philippines—became the checklist for Navarra's dish. Eighteen garden vegetables are prepared individually, through various techniques, then layered all together to resemble a potted plant. This results in an amalgamation of flavors and textures, which rise and fall with every spoonful.

While it may be the youngest on the list, Toyo has received much attention around the Philippines and beyond. To date, they've collabrated with the likes of Hong Kong's Sook, Belgian Michelin-star restaurant Hertog Jan, Singapore's Nouri, and Locavore in Bali.

The Alley at Karrivin, 2316 Chino Roces Ext., Makati
+63917 720 8630
instagram.com/toyoeatery

Wildflour Café + Bakery

Wildflour quietly opened its doors in 2012 as a no-frills café in a corner of Bonifacio Global City, but it didn't take very long for it to become a favorite among Manila diners. With no initial hype or PR push, the restaurant has become a kind of brunch mecca in the city, now at five branches and counting.

It's not hard to see why. The menu is warm and inviting, with lush breakfast offerings like the croque madam and ricotta cheese pancakes, and lunch and dinner favorites like grilled octopus salad and sweet corn agnolotti. Of course, the main event is the expanse of pastries that line every branch's bar—the whiff and presence of each gloriously crafted pastry is proof that these guys know their stuff.

The driving force behind Wildflour are Marge and Walter Manzke of L.A.'s acclaimed Republique, and Marge's sister, Ana De Ocampo, who runs the restaurants. The Manzkes have long been recognized as a formidable duo in the kitchen, with Marge being named Best Pastry Chef 2014 of LA Weekly, as well as Pastry Chef of the Year by *Eater L.A.* True to their background, bread loaves, cookies, and doughnuts typical of L.A. have made it to the Philippines, but the Wildflour team has taken on local flavors as well. Their coconut pie has garnered quite a following, because of its generous layers of coconut meat and custard, with a creme anglaise poured over its buttery upper cover.

Since opening, Wildflour has set up five more branches; Greenhills, Legazpi Village, Ortigas, Rockwell, Salcedo Village, each one as well thought-out as the other. Should more shops be on the way, it will come as no surprise. Wildflour is proving to be the restaurant series to contend with.

4th Ave. cor 26th St., Fort Bonifacio Global City, Taguig
+632 856 7600 / +63917 852 0950
instagram.com/wildflourmanila

12/10

In this day and age, it's been proven that you don't need experience to get experience. For Gab Bustos and Thea De Rivera, finding a foot in the food and beverage industry was about diving right in and opening a restaurant while still in their early 20s.
12/10 is the couple's second restaurant but it's the one that fulfilled the promise their first restaurant (The Girl & the Bull) hinted at. In 12/10, the pair are noticeably more confident in their places as chef and restaurateur. Boasting small plates of Asian fare made young and fresh, with heavy leanings towards Japanese flavors, the menu shows off Bustos's bold-faced creativity in the kitchen.

The salmon kushiyaki is possibly its most sought-after dish, with skewered and torched salmon cubes blanketed by truffle oil, aonori, curry, and a sprinkling of cornflakes. This playfulness further spills out to other dishes seamlessly.

Their drinks menu is similarly nothing to scoff at. 12/10's bar has got a lot going for it—whether through generously poured highballs, or extensively shaken gin fizzes. Trust these kids to school you on things you're missing out on.

7365 Guijo St., San Antonio Village, Makati
+63915 663 2823

Mamou

When Mamou's Malou Fores was conceptualizing her restaurant, she saw it as a place that would serve meals she might have already cooked in her own home, or dishes inspired by travels that she's taken to reinventing. What materialized is a place that's equal parts French bistro and Brooklyn diner, with a touch of Filipino home cooking.

Mamou—which has since expanded to Makati's Rockwell Power Plant (Mamou Too) and Pasig's Ayala Malls The 30th (Mamou 3.0)—makes a compelling case for striking a good balance between high and low. It's become one of the frontrunners for great steaks in Manila, cooked well each time, and paired fittingly with various side dishes. But from the same kitchen that fires up dry-aged meat—and steams live Maine lobster—also comes out reimagined Filipino household staples like duck adobo rice bowls, Kurobuta sinigang, and lamb tapa. It's a place that guarantees an option for practically every kind of diner, at any time of the day.

Here, there are no rules, because sometimes you just don't need them.

G/F Serendra, Bonifacio Global City, Taguig
+632 246 9069

MAKATI

Humming with energy and a sense of constant reinvention, Makati is always on the lookout for the next big thing.

Like many other big cities around the world, Manila's central business district manages to be both glamorous and gritty, cosmopolitan and traditional. Though many of its parts struggle to keep up with the others' glitzy reputations, when challenged by its locals to grow, the city rises to the occasion.

RETAIL & MORE

Many expatriates have made the areas surrounding Ayala Avenue their homes, and Greenbelt 5 (Ayala Center) showcases both local and international design with local specialty stores such as Noteworthy, ac+632, and Common Thread sharing the spotlight with perhaps the city's biggest selection of renowned watchmakers such as Rolex, Breguet, and Jaeger-LeCoultre, and luxury department store Adora (adora.ph), which houses international brands like Givenchy and Chloé. Right next door, the Ayala Museum (Ayala Ave. cor. Dela Rosa St., Legazpi Village; ayalamuseum.org) boasts a superb, well-curated collection of historical Philippine art, and hosts entertaining talks and workshops throughout

the year. Colin Mackay's Sala (6752 Ayala Ave. cor. Makati Ave.) offers continental cuisine to please any palate, while the beautifully designed Blackbird (Ayala Triangle Gardens, Salcedo Village) is housed in the Nielsen Tower, an architectural landmark and erstwhile airport terminal in the 1940s. Located in the vicinity, Kultura (SM Makati) breathes new life into Filipino resortwear, making it the perfect place from which to source souvenirs from artisan handicrafts to chocolate-dipped dried mangoes.

DINING

Having been primarily residential neighborhoods in the past, Legazpi Village and Salcedo Village have in recent years become go-tos for brunches, late nights, and everything in between, with cool start-ups, cafes, and restaurants on every block. Both villages are a five-minute drive or 10-minute stroll from the cluster of shopping malls on Ayala Avenue. Pepi Cubano (Tropical Palms Condominium, Gallardo St., Legazpi Village) is a favorite for its hearty Cubano sandwiches, while

KAZUNORI   PHOTO BY KAI HUANG

Cartel Coffee and Deli (119 L.P. Leviste Street, Salcedo Village) is a remarkable recent addition catering to the brunch crowd. C. Palanca St. in Legazpi is home to nightlife staples like coffee-to-cocktails The Curator, wine bar Monopole, the pub The Belle & Dragon, and the whiskey bar Mandalay. This is also where many young entrepreneurs are choosing to venture, such as the young but talented chefs behind the sophisticated eatery Made Nice Supper Club (PPI Building, Esteban St., Legazpi Village; facebook.com/madeniceph), The Girl and the Bull (Grand Midori Building, Bolanos St., Legazpi Village; thegirlandthebull. com), Vengo (103 C. Palanca St., Legazpi Village; facebook.com/todovengo), the Makati outpost of taco shop Taco Vengo, the specialty coffee roasters at the popular Yardstick (106 Esteban St., Legazpi Village; yardstickcoffee.com), and Your Local (106 Esteban St., Legazpi Village; yourlocal.ph), still one of the most in-demand tables in town and tagged by *Condé Nast Traveler* as one of the must-try restaurants in the world in 2016.

MADE NICE SUPPER CLUB   PHOTO BY JL JAVIER

LIFESTYLE

But dining isn't all that there is to do in these neighborhoods. You'll likely find Manila's stylish set rummaging through the racks of marked-down pieces from Thom Browne, Céline, Sacai, and more at the newly expanded Archives d'Homme et Femme (womenswear at Midland Offices, Gamboa St., Legazpi Village; menswear at 196 Republic Glass Building, Salcedo St. cor. Aguirre St., Legazpi Village; hommeetfemme. ph), while Back Alley Barbershop (Bautista St., Salcedo Village), on the other hand, is helping transform the grooming scene for men. Meanwhile, hip co-working spaces such as Paseo 59C (59C Paseo de Roxas Ave., Makati; facebook.com/paseo59c) offer day passes for those looking to get work done in between pockets of exploration. On weekends, reserve a morning for Legazpi and Salcedo Markets, where locals head for fresh produce and inventive eats.

HOLE IN THE WALL

PHOTO BY SONNY THAKUR

Most swear the best burger they've had in town is at Sweet Ecstasy (10 Jupiter St., Bel-Air), an unassuming, open-air joint serving up milkshakes and fries alongside the meaty main event. And for some of the best Japanese in town, you can't go wrong with the authentic Japanese restaurants in the Little Tokyo compound (2277 Chino Roces Ave.), with special mention to staples like Seryna and Kikufuji.

Don't let the odd location of Va Bene (2/F Petron, EDSA cor. Pasay Rd.), adjacent to a gas station, stop you from sampling its beloved

pasta. Of note nearby are the gated communities of Dasmarinas Village and Forbes Park that are home to some of Manila's most affluent families. Developed in the 1940s, the latter is named after the American diplomat William Cameron Forbes who served as Governor General of the Philippines from 1909 to 1913.

Not too long ago, not many would have picked Poblacion, the heart of the city's red light district, for meetings or daytime meals. That's no longer the case these days, as

HIDDEN GEM

Nestled on a street populated by car dealerships and authentic Japanese eateries, La Fuerza Compound (2241 Chino Roces Ave.) hosts an interesting variety of establishments.

Finale Art File Housing three gallery spaces under the roof of a warehouse, Finale's stable of artists runs the gamut from modern masters to emerging artists. finaleartfile.com.

W/17 A beautiful assembly of lush Filipino-made furniture, home accessories, and style tomes curated by the tastemaker Andy Vazquez-Prada. w17.com

Black Market Black Market (facebook.com/blackmarketmnl) is every hip urbanite's favorite warehouse spot for an underground clubbing experience. Also located here is the popular hidden bar Finders Keepers. Walking distance is the increasingly popular **20:20** (facebook.com/2020bar).

Pasilya 18 The new home of three contemporary art galleries, namely J Studio, Archivo 1984 (archivo1984.com), and Vinyl on Vinyl (vinylonvinylgallery. com), is Pasilya 18, which has become a place to discover blue-chip art collections, as well as emerging artists and their fresh perspectives.

SWITCHING GEARS

With a myriad dive bars and eateries vying for attention, Poblacion has emerged as a burgeoning food and nightlife destination in Makati. Here are the highlights.

BAR MATHILDE   PHOTO BY JL JAVIER

BUCKY'S   PHOTO BY JL JAVIER

Ringside Bar The area's undisputed main attraction for decades, tourists often pay a visit for the sheer novelty of the experience. *Kalayaan Ave. cor. Burgos St.; facebook.com/ringsidebarmakati*

Crying Tiger Street Kitchen

The beer and Southeast Asian street food are the main draw for patrons of this convivial eatery. *4986 P. Guanzon St.; facebook.com/officialcryingtiger*

Bucky's Everything in this intimate space is delicious and well-made, from the savory comfort food to the fudge pastries and carabao's milk soft serve. *5666 Don Pedro St.; facebook.com/buckysnotabrownie*

El Chupacabra One of the district's hottest spots for drinks and tacos, this Mexican joint was one of the first to draw diners to this part of Makati. *4986 P. Guanzon St.; facebook.com/elchupacabraph*

Tambai Through a simple but ingenious crossbreed of local street food and Japanese yakitori, Tambai has become one of the neighborhood's institutions. *5779 Felipe St.; facebook.com/tambaiph*

The Social on Ebro

Poblacion's first food park has a bar and two restaurants: Crosta, a pizzeria, and Kashmir, an Indian restaurant. The Social also hosts pop-ups for independent retail brands. *The Social, 5770 Ebro St.; facebook.com/ebrostreetsocial*

Tilde Handcraft Cafe Come for the superb cakes and sourdough bread, but also for the burgers and housemade soda. *5956 Fermina St. cor. Enriquez St.; lacasitamercedes.com*

Pineapple Lab This multidisciplinary art gallery also serves as a venue for workshops, plays, and film screenings. *6071 Palma St.; pineapplelab.ph*

La Casita Mercedes A 1939 residence transformed into a charming bed and breakfast, it's a short walk away from Rockwell Center and all the nightlife options of P. Burgos. *5956 Fermina St. cor. Enriquez St.; lacasitamercedes.com*

OTO A coffee-to-cocktails concept with one of the figures behind the acclaimed The Curator on board, Oto distinguishes itself as an audiophile's dream, boasting an impressive sound system and a growing vinyl collection. *5880 Enriquez St.; facebook.com/ototo.ph*

City Garden Cocktails coupled with sweeping views of the Makati skyline. *7870 Makati Avenue; citygarden.com*

Bar Mathilde A buzzy, unpretentious watering hole frequented by the Manila workforce on weekdays and the younger set on weekends. *8483 Kalayaan Ave.; facebook.com/mathildepoblacion*

Polilya (*5658 Don Pedro St.; facebook.com/Polilya.MNL*), **Joe's Brew** (*5834 Matilde St.; facebook.com/joesbrew*), and **The Humble Heron** (*8464 Kalayaan St.; facebook.com/thehumbleheron*) serve up a taste of an increasingly impressive local craft beer industry from Engkanto Brewery, Joe's Brew, and Juan Brew, respectively.

restaurants and dive bars have popped up left and right to the delight of city slickers seeking a change in scenery. When considering varying tastes at once, Hole in the Wall (Century City Mall, Kalayaan Ave. cor. Salamanca St., Poblacion; holeinthewall.ph), is a great dining option as it features a myriad creative concepts and chef-driven stalls in a beautiful, polished space. Further evidence of the area's ongoing gentrification can be found in the numerous exercise studios, bakeries, and cafés drawing a wide range of visitors here at various times of day. For a good workout, Ride Revolution offers indoor cycling classes above STEPS Dance Studio (Kalayaan Ave.), a performing arts school that also offers Zumba sessions. Further down that road is Rockwell Center, a posh residential neighborhood with a shopping mall and commercial complex of cafés, eateries, salons, and ritzy boutiques. Rockwell is becoming a go-to for local retail, including the ready-to-wear stores of sought-after designers Rajo Laurel and Vania Romoff, as well as the boutique Cura V (Power Plant Mall, Rockwell Center), which boasts a tight edit of jewelry, home accessories, and fashion by the most talented local designers. If you're tired from shopping, indulge in some rest, relaxation, and a pedicure at Maison by Nail Spa (Edades Tower and Garden Villas, Rockwell Center).

WATCH THIS SPACE

The Alley at Karrivin and its surrounding buildings (Karrivin Plaza, 2316 Chino Roces Avenue Ext.) comprise the newest hub for creative growth.

Aphro Living The main draw at this lifestyle boutique by gallerist Tina Fernandez is the functional art pieces from some of the Philippines's most coveted artists. *facebook.com/aphroliving*

Lanai Fresh floral arrangements are a strong suit of this two-story lifestyle store, but there are also Filipino fashion and design labels to be discovered. *lanai-manila.com*

Toyo Eatery Some have sworn that they've had the best meal in Manila here. Chef Jordy Navarra's inventive take on Filipino food is certainly worth a try. *instagram.com/toyoeatery*

The Mess Hall Among the most prolific restaurateurs in Manila, the Moment Group welcomes the public into their headquarters and the best office canteen in Manila. *facebook.com/ the.messhall*

Bellas Artes Outpost Founded by young art patron Jam Acuzar, the satellite location of Bellas Artes Projects assembles four exhibitions a year, with a non-profit model that intends to provide further exposure to deserving artists. *www.bellasartesprojects.org com*

BELLAS ARTES

PHOTO BY IAN SANTOS

WHEN IN MAKATI, IT'S IMPORTANT TO KEEP IN MIND THAT EACH OF ITS NEIGHBORHOODS HAS SOMETHING TO OFFER.

DESIGN

A 10- to 15-minute drive away from Rockwell, a street nestled between the gated communities of Bel-Air has become a go-to for interior designers, architects, and design enthusiasts for its furniture showrooms. LRI Plaza (Nicanor Garcia St., Bel-Air II) is home to a number of stores purveying furniture, design pieces, and artwork. From there, make your way to Tenant Manila (9639 Kamagong St., San Antonio Village; facebook.com/tenant.manila) a café and surfwear store found on the ground floor of a boutique hotel. In the same neighborhood, an intimate café Restock (7635 Guijo St.; facebook.com/restock.ph) is located right next to the trendy Japanese-inspired eatery 12/10 (twelveten.ph). Down the street, SaGuijo (Guijo St., San Antonio Village), has become an institution of sorts for music enthusiasts, as the country's most popular bands perform here on a regular basis. Evangelista Street (Bangkal) is a one-stop shop for thrift finds. The street has withstood the test of time and remains a treasure trove of pre-loved furniture, ceramics and pottery, and even vinyl records and art.

When in Makati, it's important to keep in mind that each of its neighborhoods has something to offer. It can sound appealing to spend a full day exploring just one of them, but to venture into as many as possible is to truly get a sense of the spirit of this ever-changing city.

TAGUIG

Taguig has received renewed interest in the last decade, thanks to the unprecedented rise of Bonifacio Global City.

Taguig has received renewed interest in the last decade, thanks to the unprecedented rise of Bonifacio Global City. It's hard to imagine that it wasn't always the bustling business district it's become today—but history tells us otherwise. Acquired in 1902 by the government of the United States, the land served as the headquarters of the Philippine division of the U.S. Army, and later the Philippine Army, after the Philippines gained independence in 1946. Only in the 1990s, after more than four decades of military occupancy, would it be subjected to urban planning—and only in the last 10 years have locals seen its development come full circle.

These days the city is home to thousands of locals and expatriates, with new buildings, malls, and hotels seemingly on the rise every other month. Its streets are modeled after New York City, making them easy to navigate and more pedestrian-friendly than most other cities in the country. With a plethora of restaurants, bars and clubs, and upscale shopping all within reasonable walking distance of each other, Taguig is giving Makati—Manila's other capital for urbanization—a run for its money.

Great first impressions are made at Vask Gallery (Clipp Center,

TAGUIG IS GIVING MAKATI— MANILA'S OTHER CAPITAL FOR URBANIZATION— A RUN FOR ITS MONEY.

FULLY BOOKED

PHOTO BY JL JAVIER

BREAK A SWEAT

Exercise studios of various persuasions are drawing in those eager to discover the next big thing in the world of fitness. That they happen to all reside in one address (*8 Forbestown Rd., Burgos Circle*) is a plus.

Electric Studio
Spinning—the workout of the moment—has become a social event here.
electricstudio.ph

Flyweight Boxing
Far from the run-of-the-mill boxing studio, the boutique boxing sessions are intimate and competitive.
flyweight.ph

L!fe Yoga
Classes are offered for both beginners and longtime practitioners, with an all-organic cafe offering healthy post-workout meals
lifeyogacenter.com

Saddle Row
While not located in Forbestown, nearby Saddle Row is notable for being one of a few workout studios to offer indoor rowing, which suits those looking to improve upper-body strength and arm definition.
2F Serenda, McKinley Parkway; saddlerow.ph

SKY'S THE LIMIT

Well-equipped to provide the space to showcase great design, Bonifacio Global City houses the world's most coveted international furniture brands.

Studio Dimensione

Carrying iconic furniture labels such as Cappellini and Fritz Hansen, Studio Dimensione purveys home and office pieces of various styles, from the colorful and whimsical to the minimalist and somber.
One Parkade, 28th St. cor. 7th Ave.; studiodimensione.weebly.com

MOs Design

This showroom houses standalone stores of BoConcept and Natuzzi as well as selections from Tom Dixon, Ligne Roset, and more. Upstairs is the art gallery, Mo_Space which describes itself as artist-centered rather than market-driven.
MOs Design Building, Bonifacio High Street, 9th Ave.; mosdesign.com.ph

Furnitalia

A major Italian furniture distributor, Furnitalia is the Philippine partner of storied European home brands such as Poltrona Frau, Giorgetti, and Cassina.
30th St. cor. Rizal Dr., Crescent Park

Philux Home

Closer to home, the family-run design label founded in the Philippines has evolved from producing furniture to purveying home accessories.
2/F Shangri-La at the Fort, 30th St. cor. 5th Ave., BGC; philux.ph

11th Ave. cor. 39th St.), where Spanish chef Chele Gonzalez and his team whip up stellar Basque cuisine (tip: its weekend brunches are made extra enjoyable with free-flowing sangria). Some swear the best meal in the city can be had there—and true enough, since 2015, it's consistently on the list of Asia's 50 Best Restaurants.

LIFESTYLE AND RETAIL

The length of Bonifacio High Street is best explored on foot. Fully Booked (B6, Bonifacio High Street; fullybookedonline.com), one of Manila's major booksellers, is a good place to start for its wide range of local and international daily newspapers. This is its flagship store, with five floors (with an event space on the top floor) of books, magazines, stationery, and other paper items, as well as a café. Nearby, National Book Store's Art Bar (G/F Serendra, McKinley Pkwy.) is a sun-drenched specialty store with a carefully curated range of coffee-table books and art supplies.

Given the city's stunning growth, some of the world's biggest hospitality brands are building five- and six-star hotels here. One of them is Shangri-La at the Fort (30th St. cor. 5th Ave., BGC; shangri-la. com/shangrilaatthefort), which also boasts a retail complex featuring the Hotel Bar, a stylish and intimate speakeasy located within Pink's Hotdogs, and Signet (facebook.com/thesignetstore), a men's fashion boutique that carries a rare, well-curated selection of European labels and even brings in Italian tailors and craftsmen a few times a year for bespoke appointments. Ladies in search of fashion labels that have little to no distribution elsewhere in the Philippines should head to Love, Candypie, better known as LCP (MDI Corporate Center, 10th Ave. cor. 39th St., BGC; shoplcp.com), a beautifully designed, light-filled boutique equipped with a champagne bar and a pool of personal shoppers to ensure a VIP shopping experience. On the other side of the style spectrum, Commonwealth (SM Aura Premier) has an unparalleled selection of independent streetwear labels waiting to be discovered.

MO_SPACE

THE BEST THING ABOUT FINDING YOURSELF IN TAGUIG IS THE MANY OPTIONS IT AFFORDS.

Disciples of dermatologists Aivee and Z Teo regularly troop to The A Institute (Burgos Park, Burgos Circle, Forbestown Rd.; facebook.com/TheAInstitute) for weekly or monthly facials and spa appointments, while those truly in the know swear by the game-changing haircuts and treatments at JuRo Salon Exclusif (Kensington Place, 1st Ave. cor. 29th St., Crescent Park West; facebook.com/ JUROSalonExclusif). For a different kind of high, there's Flying Trapeze Philippines (Federacion Dr. cor. 9th Ave., Taguig; trapeze.ph), which accepts participants of all ages and skill levels.

RESTAURANTS

For special occasions, there's chef Bruce Ricketts's Japanese Mecha Uma (RCBC Corporate Center, 25th St.), acclaimed for its superb tasting menu. Another excellent choice is Hey Handsome (Net Park, 5th Ave.), an ambitious Southeast Asian restaurant specializing in Peranakan cuisine. Also in the building, Chotto Matte (facebook.com/raintreechottomatte) has become popular for its sake, shochu, and Kakubin highballs, while

HEY HANDSOME BY SONNY THAKUR

FARMACY   PHOTO BY JL JAVIER   FOWL BREAD   PHOTO BY SONNY THAKUR

the entrance on the same floor to Manila House (manilahouseinc. com), a members-only club spectacularly designed by Belgian interior designer Gert Voorjans, hides in plain sight. The biggest branch of Manam, The Moment Group's beloved restaurant purveying modern— but still authentic—Filipino fare, can also be found within the complex, though Bonifacio Global City is also home to quite a number of international restaurant chains, from Todd English Food Hall to New York institutions Ippudo and Halal Guys. A casual homegrown concept, Fowl Bread (B3, Bonifacio High Street; fowlbread.com) claims to serve the best fried chicken sandwich in Manila, and many are in agreement. As you progress to your final course, keep in mind that all sorts of meals, fancy or otherwise, can be capped off with a universal favorite: ice cream, which is done exceptionally well—and in a memorable environment to boot—at the ice cream parlor of Farmacy (Net Lima, 24th St.; facebook.com/farmacymnl), which can be found beside the first branch of the famous Wildflour, which has since expanded and turned brunch into a religion in Manila.

NIGHT LIFE

At any time of night, for as long as you're in Bonifacio Global City, it's likely that the night is still young. This is, after all, the site of Manila's biggest and most happening clubs (that one of them is aptly named The Palace should be telling). But if partying hard isn't on the to-do list for the evening, there's a range of options from which to choose, such as Las Flores (One McKinley Place, 25th St.), Tomatito (BGC Corporate Center, 11th Ave.), and Bar Pintxos (G/F, Fairways Tower, 5th Ave.cor.McKinley Rd.) for some of the city's best options for tapas bars; LIT (G/F, Serendra) for the best selection of Japanese whiskey in town, and Bank Bar (RCBC Savings Bank Corporate Center, 26th and 25th Street, BGC; momentgroup. ph/bank-bar), a speakeasy accessed through a 7-Eleven branch populated by urban professionals. The latest additions to this landscape, if you're inclined to stay out late sans the next-day hangover, include the playful and funky yet seriously cocktail-driven dive bar Yes Please! (11th Ave. cor. 38th St., Uptown Bonifacio) and Early Night? (The Fort Strip), where you can delight in Instagrammable neon signage and an affordable drink list.

The best thing about finding yourself in Taguig is the many options it affords—and if somewhere along the way you change your mind, there will definitely be more than a few other alternatives to ensure the evening comes to an end only when you're truly ready to call it a night.

EARLY NIGHT?   PHOTO BY KAI HUANG

YES PLEASE

PHOTO BY MAJOY SISON

AT ANY TIME OF NIGHT, FOR AS LONG AS YOU'RE IN BONIFACIO GLOBAL CITY, IT'S LIKELY THAT THE NIGHT IS STILL YOUNG.

MANILA BY NIGHT

The most Catholic country in Asia also has one of the best, most varied nightlife scenes in the continent. Here's a guide to being up all night in the city.

PHOTOS BY SONNY THAKUR AND JL JAVIER

BANK BAR

Black Market / Finders Keepers

Banking on its great music selection, spacious interiors (two floors), and easy-going dress code, Black Market has been a favorite destination for Manila's young party set for some time now. It's matched by its next door neighbor, the more relaxed bar, Finders Keepers—which, thanks to its popularity, is no one's "secret" discovery anymore. Both places have an industrial feel, lit by neon lights, with Finders playing the role of inebriator and Black Market as the place to let loose.

Sabio St., Makati
+63947 342 7236 (FK) / +632 541 5965 (BM)
facebook.com/blackmarketmnl

Bank Bar

Hidden behind the storage room of a 7-Eleven, Bank Bar immediately makes an impression with its high ceilings and posh interiors, but really makes a case for itself with an extensive collection of alcohol. With so much in stock, the bar spotlights one each month and crafts cocktails around its featured intoxicant. The food here is a great excuse to visit as well. Try the Cheech Flores, a small bucket of deep fried pork ruffled fat, draped with their own concoction of pork floss.

G/F RCBC Savings Bank Corporate Center, 26th St., Bonifacio Global City, Taguig
+632 801 4862 / +63917 857 0852
momentgroup.ph/bank-bar

BANK BAR

The Curator

What used to be the back bar of a wine shop has now become a corner street destination in Legazpi Village. Placing 23rd on 2017's Asia's 50 Best Bars list, this place has an impressive cocktail menu, each one graphed according to taste and alcohol content by their lineup of award-winning bartenders. What's even more impressive is their off-menu selection— the folks behind the bar are more than capable of crafting immaculate drinks based off of customers' inclinations for the night.

134 Legazpi St. cor. Carlos Palanca St., Makati
+63916 355 4129
instagram.com/thecurator_

THE CURATOR

ABV

ABV

Past a late night burger joint's fake elevator back door lies ABV, a send-up of Prohibition-era speakeasies, complete with 1920s interiors minus the watered-down moonshine from bootleggers. Ranked 45th on Asia's 50 Best Bars of 2017, the bar displays a unique devotion to alcohol as seen in its impressive list of classic and signature cocktails. Aside from its stellar dining menu, ABV also holds perhaps the largest collection of Absinth in the city.

B/F, 22 Jupiter St. cor. Galaxy St., Makati
+63917 520 1608
instagram.com/abvph

20:20

20:20 stands out from Manila nightlife with a fresh focus on the city's growing electronic club culture. A mix of local and international DJs makes the place come alive, often with hours-long sets that keep the crowd moving. Open just four times a week, from Wednesday to Saturday, a trip here will always be a party.

20a-20b La Fuerza Plaza 1, 2241 Chino Roces Ave., Makati
+63917 634 8765

The Palace Pool Club

Many tourists go to the Philippines expecting to party
on the beach. But if you never make it out of Manila
to party on one of the country's glorious beaches, the
Palace Pool Club might be the next best thing. Bringing
the resort party experience to the city, the club is the
first of its kind in Manila, housing two swimming pools
and several bars scattered around its floor space, which
can accommodate up to 4,000 guests. Patrons can even
rent cabanas that come complete with lockers, showers,
and steam room—as well as your very own butler. On
the same compound are popular "super club" Valkyrie
and luxe lounge Revel.

9th Ave. cor. 32nd St., Bonifacio Global City, Taguig
+63917 689 8888
poolclub.thepalacemanila.com

SAGUIJO

Lit

Hidden in a corner of bustling Serendra lies Lit, a
Japanese whiskey bar that houses an impressive
collection of the liquor, from the award winning to
the obscure. The bar espouses classical bartending,
which means that drinks are given reverence—up to
the ice, which are hand carved behind the bar. The
best way to explore their extensive list, however, is
through their whiskey flights, a progressive four-drink
tasting menu that features the different Japanese
whiskey distilleries.

G/F Serendra, Bonifacio Global City, Taguig
instagram.com/litmanila
+63917 510 0014

THE PALACE POOL CLUB

SaGuijo

Right on Guijo street, this house-turned-bar is a staple for anyone out to experience the local music scene up close. Packed nights at SaGuijo mean standing in a sweaty, crowded room, a few feet from the band, with a cold bottle of beer in hand. With an eclectic list of performers, from up-and-comers to big names, the music and atmosphere of the place—sweltering at times—make the drinks taste just that much better.

7612 Guijo St., San Antonio Village, Makati
+632 897 8629

MANDALAY

SAGUIJO

Today x Future

Beside a pawnshop on a nondescript street in Cubao, Today x Future is the underground bar of choice for Manila's young creative set. Also functioning as a gallery for art and a night market for books, vinyl records, and pre-loved clothing, the bar gets full quick but the real action is streetside, where regulars drink and flirt al fresco. The music is as similarly freewheeling as the bar's clientele—in this bar, the music shuffles from disco to hip hop, from '80s pop to techno.

7-T Gen. Malvar St., Cubao, Quezon City
+63928 520 9102
instagram.com/todayxfuture

The Belle & Dragon / Mandalay

The Belle & Dragon masks itself as a brunch place in the morning, with a tasty menu in tow, only to take on the form of a laid-back bar at night. Events here range from quiz nights to guest DJs to sports night viewings. If a packed room and loud music aren't your thing, wander away to their back corridor. Past the Belle & Dragon restrooms sits an armoire which opens up to Mandalay, a speakeasy named after a Rudyard Kipling poem describing his infatuation with a Burmese woman. Like the writer, this cigar and whiskey bar offers patrons an opulent experience.

100 Carlos Palanca St., Makati
+632 625 8828
thebelleanddragon.com

THE BELLE & DRAGON

LOCAL FLAVOR

No trip to the Philippines is complete without proper acquaintance with the food, routinely described as the next big food trend in the international media. Here are six favorites—from tradition-bound classics to reinvented new school places—that might give you an idea of what the buzz is about.

Abe

Abe's food takes its cues from meals native to the province of Pampanga, which is said to have culinary roots in Spanish and Malay cooking. The bringhe—the Filipino version of the world famous arroz Valenciana—on Abe's menu, for example, is poor man's paella made with sticky rice, coconut milk, and chicken. But Pampanga is where a number of more well-known Filipino dishes have their origins, and Abe gives diners just that, through a menu comprised of classics like spicy sisig, pork sinigang, fried fish, and the classic kare-kare.

G/F Serendra, Bonifacio Global City, Taguig
+632 856 9526
ljcrestaurants.com.ph

Manam

Manam is probably the only Filipino restaurant that serves the full range of classic, well-known, local dishes, side-by-side with a modern take on each one. The iconic sinigang is listed for those that opt for having it the standard way, but there is also the watermelon sinigang with short ribs, which is sour yet sweet all at once. Manam also allows diners to pick dishes out in small, medium, and large sizes, which is grounds for tasting a full range of their offerings, no matter how big a group your party is.

G/F Net Park Building, 5th Ave., Bonifacio Global City
+632 332 9390
momentgroup.ph/manam-comfort-filipino

Locavore

Reinventing Filipino food might be difficult, but Locavore manages to do just that, by flaunting their playfulness through the dishes they serve. Filipino food here departs from convention; the sinigang, for instance, drops the clear broth for a thick and sour gravy, its elements sizzling on a pan. Not to be missed is their sisig made of battered oysters, which bursts with umami at every bite.

10 Brixton St., Kapitolyo, Pasig
+63917 621 8909
locavore.ph

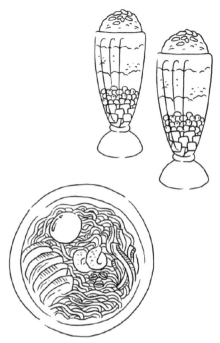

Milky Way Cafe

It started out as an ice cream parlor in the 1960s that later branched out to become a full-fledged Filipino restaurant and eventually became a Manila institution. Milky Way is an all-around diner with all the classic local dishes you need to know, from the lumpia and kare-kare, down to the halo-halo you shouldn't leave without trying. The group behind Milky Way has also taken it upon themselves to create pre-packed, blast-frozen food as a meal solution for those that want to heat their meals up at home.

2/F Milkyway Building, 900 Arnaiz Ave. cor.
Paseo de Roxas, Makati
cafe.milkywayrestaurant.com
+632 843 4124

Sarsa

More than offering just widely recognized Filipino food, the popular chain Sarsa has distinguished itself among Manila's Filipino restaurants by introducing the city to the regional flavors of Negros, a province located down south. A staple from that part of the country is a noodle soup called batchoy, which Sarsa has created its own version of—bone broth with the taste of garlic seeping out is layered with egg noodles, marrow, meat slivers, pork cracklings, and a fresh yolk waiting to be popped. Other must-try dishes from Negros served in Sarsa are the chicken inasal, sizzling kansi, and pancit molo.

The Forum, 7th Ave. cor. Federacion Dr., Bonifacio
Bonifacio Global City, Taguig
+632 866 0912
instagram.com/sarsakitchen

Tambai

One of the early settlers in the now food-crazy Poblacion neighborhood, Tambai initially served as a respite for drunk—or soon-to-be-drunk-customers from neighboring bars looking for something salty to balance out the alcohol. Its simple crossbreed of local street food and Japanese yakitori—Filipino yakitori, essentially—immediately gained a devoted following in a relatively short amount of time. What was once a small shack sharing its space with a neighborhood variety store has turned into a full-fledged bar and restaurant. With its casual vibe and reasonably priced items, Tambai makes for a great place to drink, hang out, and munch on skewers.

5779 Felipe St., Poblacion, Makati
+63917 724 4654
facebook.com/TambaiPH

EATING EVERYWHERE

In mall-obsessed Manila, you're going to find a few establishments pop up consistently. Here's a guide to well-loved local restaurant chains.

Aristocrat

Years before wartime in Manila, Lola Asiang, the matriarch of the Reyes family, decided that she wanted to turn the first floor of her family home into a canteen that made affordable Filipino food. First serving lumpia, dinuguan and puto, and arroz caldo, the place grew to serve adobo-filled pressed sandwiches for diners on the go. Continuing the business when the war ended, she found a way to lessen the use of cutlery through chicken barbecue on a stick, marinated in a sweet and nutty sauce, served with java rice (cooked with turmeric and annatto), which would eventually become the restaurant's signature dish. Traditional Filipino food is on the menu, but for a taste of its history, the adobo flying saucer remains on the list, as well as the chicken barbecue with java sauce and rice. It's the place that has options for any budget, because Lola Asiang believed you don't need a lot to eat like an aristocrat.

aristocrat.com.ph

Cibo

Cibo came at a time when eating the cuisines of other countries was thought to be reserved for red letter days or, simply, too costly. Cibo, the brainchild of 2016 Asia's Best Female Chef Margarita Fores, was the antithesis to this, as authentic Italian food was served in a casual setting, and at approachable prices. Its current menu isn't far off from what it served when its first shop opened: sandwiches, pastas, pizzas, and dips—a lot of which have earned the chain a loyal fanbase through the years. Cibo favorites include a tomato-based pasta with strings of melted mozzarella called the Al Telefono, toast with spinach and cheese dip, and the classic Italian margherita pizza. While other Italian restaurants have opened over the years, Cibo has managed to reinvent itself while maintaining its mission of creating accessible, yet authentic Italian dishes.

cibo.ph

Goldilocks

Goldilocks is a fool-proof bakeshop that dates back to the '60s. Initially just a cake shop, Goldilocks eventually branched out to make other desserts, which still echo the era of its beginnings: mocha rolls, a crumbly shortbread called polvoron, cathedral windows jelly, and the iconic crema de fruta. The growth of Goldilocks made it convenient for tasty and nicely decorated sweets to be purchased without prior notice, at prices that didn't burn a hole in the pocket. They've since expanded to serve simple Filipino food, which are equally appetizing as the sweets that have built their empire.

goldilocks.ph

Mary Grace

Mary Grace Dimacali's hobby for baking cakes is what eventually led her to create her own take on the Filipino pastries ensaymada and cheese rolls. A regular at annual Christmas bazaars, the success and wide reach of her pastries led her to open a few kiosks and, eventually, a string of Mary Grace Cafes. Each space is decorated like a home, abundant in wooden furnishings, and peppered with framed photos on the wall and handwritten notes under every table top. The meals are as hearty as the cafe: classic Filipino breakfasts of longganisa, tapa, or tocino with eggs, and standard cafe fare of salads and pastas. A visit here shouldn't go without a taste of the things that started it all, the ensaymada and the cheese roll. Mary Grace's grilled ensaymada dunked into thick and nutty hot chocolate is a bite right into Christmas, which, if you're in a Mary Grace, can be experienced the whole year 'round.

marygracecafe.com

Max's Fried Chicken

The idea for Max's was born after the second World War, when Maximo Gimenez befriended GIs stationed around Quezon City who would stop by his place for a free drink. The growing number of soldiers that would stop by prompted him to open his own restaurant, hence Max's, which started off by serving fried chicken—an American staple—cooked a different way. Perhaps it was the chicken's tender flesh, or its crisp skin sans the thick coat of batter, that earned Max's a cult following. Whatever it is, the "House that Fried Chicken Built," has gone on to have shops across the country, and as far away as the US and Canada.

maxsfriedchicken.com

Jollibee

During Anthony Bourdain's visit to the country, one of his first sightings was at a Jollibee, feasting on Chickenjoy and sweet noodles. Needless to say a taste of the local food scene isn't complete without a bite from this bug. Jollibee has managed to become the top fast food brand in the Philippines, surpassing even global chains present in the country. Its dishes are a mix of Filipino food on a budget—such as the pancit palabok and breakfast rice meals—and more western elements like fried chicken, hamburger, and spaghetti. With the latter, however, Jollibee has intentionally attuned its flavors to suit the Filipino palate, particularly the spaghetti with its bits of red hotdog and sweet tomato sauce. Its popularity has propelled the brand into global status, with stores in the US, Vietnam, Hong Kong, and Qatar. It's fast food for sure—but Jollibee has definitely become an icon of Philippine dining.

jollibee.com.ph

THE SOUTH

Parañaque, Muntinlupa, and Las Piñas—these cities
that collectively comprise the south of Metro Manila
may seem out of the way, but its varied haunts and
lesser-known gems prove worth discovering.

Parañaque, Muntinlupa, and Las Piñas collectively comprise the south of Manila, and while Parañaque isn't even an hour from Makati—it can take less than half an hour on a good day, in fact—its locals have been granted a stereotype, as residents of these cities are famously averse to venturing too far outside their neighborhoods. As such, they've gotten crafty by building their own little world within the confines of their neighborhoods.

RESTAURANTS

For an extensive selection of organic food items, head to healthy grocer Real Food (Molito Lifestyle Mall, Alabang), which purveys everything from kale chips and almond butter to organic meats and fresh produce. Brera (Molito Commercial Compound, Commerce Ave. cor. Madrigal Ave., Alabang; facebook.com/brera-molito) is a great source of bread and other deli goods, such as steaks, cheese, and cold cuts.

Alabang is home to some of Manila's finest authentic Spanish cuisine thanks to the original branch of Miguel Vecin's tapas bar Bar Pintxos (Don Gesu Building, Don Jesus Blvd., Cupang; facebook.com/barpintxos), and The Black Pig (Commercenter, Commerce Ave. cor. Filinvest Ave., Alabang; theblackpigbar.com), a bar and restaurant known for its European fare and assortment of charcuterie, helmed by Spanish chef Carlos Garcia. For dessert, there's crisp churros and hot chocolate inspired by their authentic Spanish

ALABANG IS HOME TO SOME OF MANILA'S FINEST AUTHENTIC SPANISH CUISINE

REAL FOOD

PHOTO BY MIGUEL NACIANCENO

counterparts at La Maripili (Alabang Town Center), which also offers croissants and toast for breakfast.

While ramen joints have popped up left and right throughout Manila, non-southerners have been known to make the trip to Alabang solely for Yushoken (Molito Commercial Complex) and its tonkotsu shoyu ramen. Veteran caterer Neil Ramos' Neil's Kitchen (Westgate, Filinvest City) is similarly beloved for its polished take on Filipino food and its beautiful Mediterranean-inspired site. There's also Elbert's Sandwiches (Commercenter, Commerce Ave. cor. Filinvest Ave., Alabang), a more casual offshoot of Elbert Cuenca's famed Elbert's Steak Room.

RETAIL

On the shopping front, one must stop over at STYLE (737 Roxas Blvd., Baclaran, Parañaque; vizcarra1925.com) on the way to or from the south, for handmade bags and other accessories designed by Rita Nazareno, whose intricate and unique designs are also sold—and highly coveted—in fashion capitals such as Tokyo, New York, Paris, and Italy.

MUSIC SCENE

Though admittedly out of the way for most Manila folk, 19 East (East Service Road, Sucat, Muntinlupa; 19east.com) remains one of the metro's premier music destinations. Many of the country's most well-loved OPM musicians—from fixtures

LA CHINESCA   PHOTO COURTESY OF JAE PICKRELL

of the '90s and early aughts such as Side A, to current superstars like Up Dharma Down, to rising talents—regularly headline live music offerings at the venue.

Just before you're ready to make your way home, cap off the evening with a skyline view of Alabang and Las Piñas at The Nest at Vivere Hotel (Filinvest City; viverehotel.com.ph), where you can dine poolside 30 stories up in the air and feel like you're worlds away from the hustle and bustle of Manila.

LOCALS HAVE GOTTEN CRAFTY BY BUILDING THEIR OWN LITTLE WORLD WITHIN THE CONFINES OF THEIR NEIGHBORHOODS.

ON THEIR TURF

Once upon a time, BF Homes wasn't top of mind for diners looking for the hottest new restaurant. That has certainly changed.

Jang Ga Nae

One of the oldest Korean spots on this side of the city remains a favorite of locals. *237 Aguirre Ave., Parañaque*

Sensei Sushi

Chef Bruce Ricketts's first restaurant seats only 20, but many have become loyal patrons throughout the years. *268 Aguirre Ave., Parañaque; facebook.com/senseiph*

Mama Lou's Italian Kitchen

Located along one of BF Homes's quieter streets is this restaurant celebrated for its pizza, pasta, and escargot. *Tropical Ave. cor. Palace St., BF International, Las Piñas*

Hanakazu

Fresh sashimi and sushi plus other authentic Japanese dishes that are worth the hefty price tag. *108 Aguirre Ave., Parañaque*

Magnum Opus

A hole-in-the-wall cafe and art gallery doing third-wave coffee right. *The Prime Building, 115 Aguirre Ave., Parañaque; facebook.com/magnumopusfinecoffees*

La Chinesca

Also from young culinary talent Bruce Ricketts, who can seem to do no wrong, this 19-seat Mexican eatery is dishing out some of the finest tacos in the city. *248 Aguirre Avenue, BF Homes; facebook.com/lachinesca*

Manila

Manila is a difficult area to manage
but it has its hidden charms —
and discovering those charms
can be a magical moment. When
one punctuates it with its locals'
stories, warmth, and raw panorama,
the experience becomes even richer.

EDITED BY DON JAUCIAN

Why OLD MANILA is New Again

BY MARIKA CONSTANTINO

I always tell them: It takes special people to love Manila.

For decades, Old Manila—the catch-all phrase that has come to mean Intramuros (the actual Old Manila), Binondo, Escolta, the area surrounding Malacañang Palace—has been regarded as a place whose time has already passed. It seemed like the rest of Metro Manila had moved on to newer, shinier cities. What use do we have for the old city?

In recent years, a new generation of dreamers and creatives have made it their life's work to answer that question—and so far, what's passed for answers has been nothing but encouraging.

Revitalization is an often used word when it comes to Escolta, the street 98B Collaboratory—an artist-run initiative where I serve as executive director—calls home. While older generations recall the street with with fondness and nostalgia, younger folk think of it as something archaic—too far from the business district of Makati to invest in, too set in its ways for the hyper-developed Fort Bonifacio.

> One cannot help but fall in love with the area——the history that unfolded, the character it represents, the possibilities for the future.

But at one point, Escolta was Manila's main commercial borough. Structures designed by some of the country's most important architects rose here. Imported items, stylish clothing, and the most luxurious goods could all be found here. Today, the street that was once the city's upscale district has been mired in a series of unfortunate events spanning through several decades—World War II, the emergence of other big cities around Manila, and the relocation of big business to other locales. This has left Escolta a mere shadow of its former glory.

When 98B Collaboratory relocated to Escolta in 2012, some considered the move foolish. What is a group that organizes activities, events, exhibitions, and programs in relation to contemporary art practice going to do in a neighborhood that, while historic, has long been culturally barren and just too out of the way from the rest of Manila's art scene? It starts with appreciating Escolta. We appreciate the heritage that is imbued in its structures, the

countless narratives that we hear from various people and within it, the community's latent nature to adapt, evolve and invigorate itself. While its recent state may feel like a lost cause for a lot of people, for artists and creatives like us, we see so much beauty and potential.

One cannot help but fall in love with the area—the history that unfolded, the character it represents, the possibilities for the future. We consider Escolta our home. This is our playground.

A few months after moving to Escolta, we started our artist residency program, inviting friends and acquaintances we'd met in exhibits and similar residencies abroad and opening up our little corner of Manila to the rest of the world.

At the start of those residencies, I always tell them: It takes special people to love Manila. The first impressions are pretty consistent—the traffic, the heat, the chaos, the lack of system. And that's fair. Manila's not an easy place to navigate. A certain amount of openness to the misadventure is required, if you're ever going to appreciate it. But I believe that if you can find it in you to be a little more open, to be flexible, and to be adaptable, suddenly Manila will unlock itself to you. You'll discover its charms, its hidden treasures—the people and the history, the horror vacui along with the absurd horrors, the kitschy and the breathtaking. And you see people who are always trying to make their lives better. You see people who always manage to find a reason to be happy about things. Things are unlocked.

I think part of the discovery of Manila is through the local's eyes—and I don't think that's hard. Filipinos are very

       PHOTO BY JL JAVIER

FIRST UNITED BUILDING

friendly. Filipinos inherently love the country. I think when things are seen through a local's resourcefulness, resilience, then a certain level of appreciation is always unearthed. It's true. Despite all its failures, despite the strange political scenario we're in at the moment—whichever side of the political coin we're on—I think there's genuine love. There's genuine optimism and there's genuine hope. I think when foreigners see that, that's when things are further appreciated.

Manila is a difficult area to manage but it has its hidden charms—and discovering those charms can be a magical moment. When one punctuates it with its locals' stories, warmth, and raw panorama, the experience becomes even richer. I think most of our residents have seen that. They have discovered the system within the non-system—because there is.

We do realize that it's an uphill climb to put Escolta back on the map. Coupled with the objective of making art more accessible to the general public, it can be a daunting task at times. But the desire to generate more awareness keeps us in 98B and the rest of the growing family of creatives who call Escolta home, motivated.

What happens when the memories and recollections of a certain place end with those who were privileged enough to experience it during its prime? Should it just be relegated to the past and merely cast away? Save it for a history lesson or a field trip? Heritage shouldn't just be about nostalgia. It's also about what can be done with the memories and mistakes of the past, applying all these things to try and

celebrate the fact that we can look at it through a new lens. Heritage doesn't just have to mean museum-like. Sometimes, the understanding of nostalgia ends with conservation and preservation—keeping things as it once was—it becomes boring. This is exactly what we're trying not to do in Escolta.

It's important to connect with the generation now. Otherwise, if they just see something like Escolta as something static, then that's that. It can't just be nostalgia. The idea is to continuously build new memories and new experiences. Because then, this place will be as important to this generation as it was to their parents or grandparents. Because they experienced something there. Because they made a memory there.

Make it dynamic. Make it active. Make it alive. Your energy is needed for the regeneration.

Marika Constantino is the executive director of 98B Collaboratory. She says she is continually striving to strike the balance between the cerebral, conceptual and experiential aspects of art with life in general, thus, fueling her passion for artistic endeavors. Visit 98-b.org for more details on 98B Collaboratory.

Old Manila

The sweltering, throbbing heart of Manila lies in the arteries and small pockets of the capital's proper— colonial era buildings, a whole "belt" of schools, makeshift shelters, vibrant structures where culture and heritage are on full display.

One way to look at the rich and colorful melange of culture in the streets of Old Manila is by way of an art biennale, musician David Byrne suggested, visiting the Philippines to do research for his Imelda Marcos-inspired Off-Broadway production *Here Lies Love*. The sweltering, throbbing heart of Manila lies in the arteries and small pockets of the capital's proper—a daisy chain of colonial era buildings, a whole "belt" of schools, makeshift shelters stacked up on one another, and, if you look closely, vibrant structures where culture and heritage are on full display.

The hotels are located right next to some of the most historic enclaves in Manila.

Accommodations

There are a few options to stay in the Old Manila area, especially in the Malate area, but two quintessential hotels are Bayleaf Hotel (Muralla St., Intramuros; thebayleaf.com.ph), which offers a great view of the city from its 10th floor rooftop bar; and Manila Hotel (One Rizal Park; manila-hotel.com.ph), which has been around

for over a hundred years and has seen its share of visitors—from General Douglas MacArthur (after whom an eight-room suite in the hotel has been named) to the Beatles.

Historic Landmarks

These hotels are located right next to some of the most historic enclaves in Manila: the walled city of Intramuros (intramuros.gov.ph), and Luneta Park complex (Roxas Boulevard, Ermita, Manila; npdc.gov.ph) that spans the National Museum (1000 Padre Burgos Ave.; nationalmuseum.gov.ph), which houses a collection of Filipino classical and contemporary art, including the massive *Spoliarium* by Juan Luna; the monument of the national hero, Jose Rizal; the National Museum of National History, and swathes of greenery perfect for lounging while waiting for the sunset in Manila Bay.

The cobblestoned streets of Intramuros provide a gateway to the country's Spanish colonial past, from the dungeons of Fort Santiago to the

ecclesiastical grandeur of Manila Cathedral (Sto. Tomas, Intramuros), which has survived World War II bombings and is now host to the Papal Mass whenever the Catholic pope is in the country. Restaurants can also be found in Intramuros, such as Illustrado (744 Gen. Luna St.; illustradorestaurant.com.ph), which serves the curious sampaguita-flavored ice cream. A few blocks away is Bahay Tsinoy Museum (32 Anda St., Intramuros; bahaytsinoy.org), a good stop to glean an understanding of the Chinese-Filipino relations that have forged on for centuries. The sunset can also be viewed on the walls overlooking the Intramuros golf course, which also has a level-view of the nearby Art Deco and neo-classical structures that provide a glimpse of Filipino ingenuity. Explore the area while the sun is low.

Old Manila Food Trip

Lunch calls for Binondo, famously known as the oldest Chinatown in the world. Try any of the authentic Chinese restaurants or even the Estero Fast Food (Ongpin St.,

The cobblestoned streets of Intramuros provide a gateway to the country's Spanish colonial past.

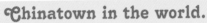

Lunch calls for Binondo, famously known as the oldest Chinatown in the world.

Binondo), where you can feast on frog legs. If you have a few hours to spare, sign up for the three-hour Binondo Food Wok (oldmanilawalks.com) to immerse yourself in the sights and tastes of the area—Anthony Bourdain is one of the many travelers who have taken this tour. If you're up for a different kind of Asian cuisine, Quiapo (Quezon Blvd., Quiapo) has several Maranao and Tausug restaurants. As the streets can be quite the labyrinth, the company of a local guide is ideal.

Art and Culture

Religious architecture spread around the area boasts quite an impressive lineup, such as the Gothic Revival San Sebastian Church (Pasaje del Carmen Street, Quiapo), the country's

only all-steel church that Alexandre Gustave Eiffel was rumored to have been involved in the building of. The Chinese Cemetery (Sta. Cruz, Manila) is another site for historic, flamboyant, and sometimes out-of-this-world funerary architecture; then take a leisurely stroll around the circular gardens of Paco Park (Belen St., Paco, Manila), the city's former municipal cemetery now popularly used as a reception venue for concerts and weddings.

In the afternoon, head to cultural destinations around the area, such as the Solidaridad Bookshop (531 Padre Faura St.; facebook.com/solidaridad-bookshop), run by the writer F. Sionil Jose, who has been tipped to win the Nobel Prize more than a few times; Cinematheque Center Manila (885 Kalaw Avenue, Ermita; fdcp.ph) for films by master Filipino auteurs and film festivals; and the colonial mansion home of 1335Mabini (Casa

Tesoro, 1335 Mabini St, Ermita; 1335mabini.com) and Museum of Contemporary Art and Design (De La Salle-College of Saint Benilde School of Design and Arts, Dominga St., Malate; mcadmanila.org.ph) for your art fix.

—DON JAUCIAN

BINONDO CHINATOWN
PHOTO BY TAMMY DAVID

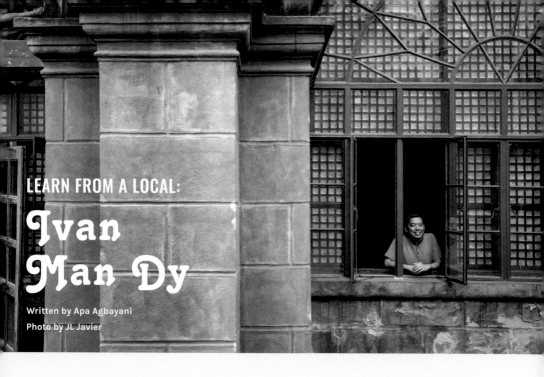

Ivan Man Dy

Written by Apa Agbayani
Photo by JL Javier

To Man Dy, every place is a piece in the fascinating jigsaw puzzle of Manila's history.

Few people are as familiar with Manila's nooks and crannies as Ivan Man Dy. The founder of specialist tour outfit Old Manila Walks has lived his entire life in the city, having grown up in Binondo and studied in Malate and Sampaloc. "I'm a Manila boy through and through," he says.

His love for the city, coupled with his background as a museum docent, led Man Dy to develop the concept of Old Manila Walks. "My biggest museum, essentially, is the city. Not in a very conventional, air-conditioned, curated sense, but the very streets, the buildings," he says.

Man Dy tailors each of Old Manila Walks' tours to the city's various neighborhoods, taking into consideration each one's stories, attractions, and nuances. The tours include a beginner's course on Manila history in Intramuros, a

political history tour through San Miguel, which includes Malacañang Palace, a food trip through Binondo's high-density commercial spaces, and a spine-tingling walk through the Chinese Cemetery.

To Man Dy, every place is a piece in the fascinating jigsaw puzzle of Manila's history. "It's a very multi-ethnic story. That is something that most people don't really see for some reason—that you have different neighborhoods that are totally different from each other, and all of them have their roles to play in the development of the city," he says.

An essential part of the tours is that Man Dy leads guests on foot, offering an unfiltered experience of its sights, sounds, and smells. Through his tours, Man Dy hopes to give a full picture of the city's rich history. "I'm very much into the heritage of the place—the old buildings, the architecture, the food, the traditions," he says, singling out Manila's stunning architecture as an example.

"I think Manila is one of the great art deco cities in the region, but unfortunately people don't appreciate it as much because we keep tearing down old buildings," he says. "That is what we try to give people in our tours—a deeper understanding of this whole story and this whole heritage of Manila, at least in the two, three hours that we're with them."

7 of Manila's Architectural Wonders

It has been said that Philippine architecture reflects the struggle to define the Filipino identity. A quick survey of Manila's most impressive buildings bear influences that come from the world over—various permutations of classical, neoclassical, art deco, brutalist forms—tailor-fit to the climate and requirements of living in a tropical country. The blueprint of Filipino homes can be traced back from the era of bahay kubo, to the Spanish-introduced style of bahay na bato (house of rocks), to today's post-modern style—variations of which still exist in the city today. The practicality that pervaded the aesthetic of the early forms of architecture have been carried over by some of the country's best architects in their more remarkable works, keeping in mind that these structures will be subject to the extremes of Philippine climate and the burden of human wear and tear, while still serving as a monument to the ideals and aspirations of the time.

The city gives off an immediate impression of being a dizzying megalopolis—high-rises and sprawling arteries greet you upon landing. But farther into the capital itself, the colonial past of the country comes alive. An ideal jump-off point would be Kilometer Zero in Manila's Luneta Park. Branch off at any point and there is an architectural gem waiting to be discovered. Though age-worn, there is much beauty in their ruin.

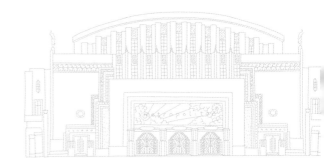

Manila Metropolitan Theater

A masterwork of architect Juan Arellano, the Manila Metropolitan Theater (Antonio Villegas Street, Ermita, Manila) was originally conceived as a venue for operas, Broadway reproductions, and orchestral concerts. Though its current form is a decimated shell of its former glory, some of its most remarkable details are still intact. During its heyday, the building was constructed as a passionate tribute to the arts, with crystal lamps made from bamboo stalks, murals by National Artist Fernando Amorsolo, iron-wrought gates resembling leaves, and sculptures of Adam and Eve by Italian artist Francesco Riccardo Monti.

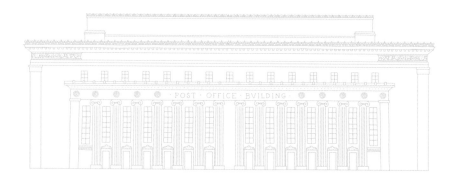

Manila Post Office

The Manila Post Office (Liwasang Bonifacio, Magallanes Drive, Intramuros, Manila) is another neoclassical marvel built in the 1920s. It is a result of a collaboration between three architects: Juan Arellano, Tomas Mapua, and Ralph Doane, and is part of famed urban planner Daniel Burnham's vision of making Manila a "Paris on the Prairie." The structure is a work of monumental symmetry: the rectangular main building is fronted by 14 Ionic columns on top of a wide set of stairs, bookended by two semicircular wings.

National Museum

The National Museum (1000 Padre Burgos Avenue, Ermita, Manila) is an imposing structure that is home to some of the best works of classical and modern art by Filipino masters. The pastel-colored building was originally built as a public library in 1926 but was then used by the Senate and the House of Representatives during the Commonwealth era. Like most of the buildings in the city, it was a casualty of the carpet bombings during the World War II. Its current form as a treasure trove of visual arts only date back since 2003, a product of a P20 million renovation project. The high-ceilinged Senate Hall has been restored to its pre-war eminence and below it is the old Congress Hall which is where Juan Luna's *Spoliarium* is now on display.

El Hogar Filipino

Right across a string of buildings along the Pasig River is the El Hogar Filipino (Escolta St., Sta. Cruz, Manila), an endangered structure that has been subject of many advocacies aiming to preserve the city's architectural heritage. Its style is a fusion of renaissance elements (arched windows and ironwork details in the staircase) and classical revival (symmetrical details and patterns apparent in its entirety). It was built around the early 1900s as a five-story office building. It has been threatened with demolition numerous times since it was sold to a new owner but the strong petition from heritage conservationists might still save it from such a fate.

Manila Cathedral

Inside the walls of Intramuros is a grand exemplar of colonial structures still existing in the country: the Manila Cathedral (Cabildo St. cor. Beaterio St., Intramuros, Manila). The minor basilica has been around since 1571 and has survived catastrophes, including several earthquakes, and was reduced to rubble during the Battle of Manila in 1945 and then subsequently rebuilt. Its façade is made up of numerous elements, including bronze panels paying tribute to the Blessed Virgin Mary and six statues of famous saints. Inside is a grandiose choir loft with a four-manual organ, and a half-orange dome with stained glass windows the Filipino artist Galo Ocampo.

Far Eastern University

Another architectural marvel is the Far Eastern University building (Nicanor Reyes St., Sampaloc Manila). The campus, by National Artist for Architecture Pablo Antonio, is one of the largest surviving collections of art deco in the country. It is also a living museum in itself, housing works by Filipino artists such as paintings by Fernando Amorsolo, a chapel tile mosaic by Vicente Manansala, a sculpture by Napoleon Abueva, and a mural by Carlos "Botong" Francisco. It was awarded the UNESCO Asia Pacific Heritage award for Cultural Heritage in 2005.

National Theater of the Cultural Center of the Philippines

Perhaps one of the most controversial of all of Manila's structures is the Tanghalang Pambansa (national theater) of the Cultural Center of the Philippines (Roxas Blvd., Pasay). Built to resemble a traditional bahay na bato, it sits on 77 hectares of reclaimed land as part of former first lady Imelda Marcos's massive project of venues for artistic performances. It is a Brutalist structure by architect Leandro V. Locsin embedded with a history of political power play and intrigue, having been called a "fascist building" owing to its association with the Marcos family. Today, it remains a venue for theatrical presentations, film festivals, and art shows.

Escolta

After a few decades in decay, Manila's former
financial district is once again thriving—thanks
to a creative community that's making heritage
a living, breathing thing.

Once Manila's bustling financial district in the heart of Binondo, Escolta has spent a few decades in decay, its old neoclassical and Art Deco spaces gathering dust, with the occasional heritage site getting the bulldozer.

Architectural Wonders

Many of the street's architectural wonders remain intact. You can still see the labyrinthine arcade of El Hogar Filipino Building (Juan Luna St. cor. Muelle dela Industría St.), or the magnificent façade of the Don Roman Santos Building (Plaza Lacson cor. Escolta St.), which was once the main ofice of the Bank of the Philippine Islands. There is also the Calvo Building (266 Escolta St.), which is home to the Escolta Museum.

Art and Culture

These days, a handful of Manila's young creative startups are breathing life into the street's historic spaces. First to arrive was 98B COLLABoratory (98-b.org), a multidisciplinary art laboratory that set up shop at the mezzanine floor of the First United Building (413 Escolta Street). Apart from holding regular talks and workshops, the team set up the First United Building Community Museum—which commemorates the life of Sy Lian Teng, the man who revitalized the Perez Samanillo Building and along with it the district's rich history—as well as the retail playground HUB: Make Lab (First United Building; 98-b.org/hubmakelab).

Many of the street's architectural wonders remain intact.

Envisioned as an incubator for creative startups, HUB is home to 22 stalls—some of which change from time to time—including Gen. Mdse (facebook.com/GENMDSE), a selection of Manila-made products from apparel to paper crafts and pre-packaged edibles. Upstairs is First Coworking Community (5/F First United Building; facebook.com/firstcoworkingmnl), a coworking space.

For a cup of the neighborhood's best espresso, you can head to The Den (facebook.com/TheDenManila), also within the First United Building. The coffee shop was designed with minimal intervention to showcase the historic building's grit. For some of the best local craft beer and a bowl of lechon rice served Hainanese-style, there's Fred's Revolución (fredsrevolucion.com) on the same floor.

Among the other creative tenants of the First United Building

are design collective 1/0 (5/F, First United Building; facebook.com/1.0designcollective) who are at the helm of the district's recent architectural initiatives; VivaManila (vivamanila.org), a nonprofit organization dedicated to revitalizing Manila through art and culture; Kalsada Coffee (4/F First United Building; kalsada.com) which champions Philippine specialty coffee and fair trade; The Public School Manila (5/F, First United Building; publicschoolmnl.com), a studio which does design work primarily for government agencies. Public School also houses the concept store Standard Objects, which carries a selection of books, local and international magazines, and craft works by young artists; and Manila Who (G/F, First United Building; manilawho.wixsite.com/manilawho) which offers scavenger hunt-type historical tours of the neighborhood.

— APA AGBAYANI

98B COLLABORATORY

CONVERSATIONS:

Robert and Lorraine Sylianteng

First United Building owners Robert and Lorraine Sylianteng have been instrumental to Escolta's revival, thanks to their willingness to share space and collaborate with the creative companies in their building.

Did you have any hesitations or apprehensions opening up the building to creative companies?

Before the creatives came, Escolta was dead on weekends and after-office hours. Most of our tenants were into ports-related or lending businesses. We had great apprehension opening up the building to creatives. First of all, the building is owned by Robert's four siblings, too. We didn't know how they would feel that we were going a very different direction.

Then we invited 98B to come over. It was not an easy road. Slowly, we learned mutual trust and understanding by taking baby steps. As businessmen, we always tell Marika [Constantino of 98B] that we don't quite understand their art but are slowly learning!

How do you approach this collaborative relationship with your creative tenants?

Our relationships with our past tenants were developed over the past 40 years and have been mostly cut and dry. With creatives, events are very fluid and require an open mind and inclusive heart. It was difficult to understand at the beginning. It almost felt like we had a baby and had a big generation gap, but we learned to adjust.

Before, our hours were strictly 7:00 A.M. to 7:00 P.M. However, with creatives, you can't dictate their time, so we've been more accommodating with their hours. Actually, they have blanket permission to stay in the building to their heart's content.

How would you describe the growth you've witnessed at First United and the rest of Escolta in the last few years?

In the past one or two years, we've experienced an upsurge of people who want to rent from us. I think it's because of all the "noise" they hear from our creatives. We are very grateful for that. And it's not just our building; it's also the other Escolta buildings. The next big task is to infect all the other building owners to take in more creatives in their buildings. They should try it! It's a great joyride.

ARTS SERRANO

CONVERSATIONS:

Arts Serrano

of 1/o design collective

One of the minds behind Escolta's revival is architect Angelo Ray Serrano, who is spearheading a handful of initiatives to redefine heritage spaces in the city.

How do you reinvent a space like First United Building?

A project we worked on is a co-working space. One thing we look at is what's there in the space that shows much of the history of the building, how it progressed from the war, and what survived afterwards. When we tore down parts of the ceiling, we saw some details that were kept hidden. We tried to highlight certain elements that define the space, but one of the things we think about when designing in old spaces is how to connect old spaces to the younger generation because there's a disconnect. We just want to show that places like this can be invaded—they can be taken over and used in ways that are relatable to our generation.

What are the challenges of working as an architect when the concept of heritage conservation is undervalued?

We're very market-driven and I think it's a very challenging environment. We're all about selling spaces, even when you're making something really fake. As architects, one of our overarching rules is to raise awareness [on heritage conservation], specifically in Escolta. All the events we're putting up are geared toward connecting people who don't have much appreciation of our heritage, but we want them to be part of what we're doing here, and indirectly influence them to be more aware about the importance of Escolta.

In Manila, you don't really see anything like this apart from Intramuros or some parts of Malate or Ermita. This shows our constant attempt to define Manila as a design city. Even if you see much of the European references here, it's all part of trying to define how we are as a nation, so when we tear down, say, the PNB building, we tear down a part of our face, because that's already part of our definition. In a way, that's one overarching goal we have—to raise awareness about heritage.

FIRST UNITED BUILDING

LEARN FROM A LOCAL:

Carlos Celdran

The *New York Times* has a tip in case you're planning to visit the Philippines: "There are tour guides, and there are tour guides. Should you visit the Philippines, see if you can still get Carlos Celdran..."

One of the most polarizing figures in the Philippines, Carlos Celdran is nonetheless Manila's premier tour guide. His official disclaimer says: "This is performance art in the guise of a walking tour." But throughout his two-hour Walk This Way tour of Intramuros, which takes you through the origins of Manila, the Spanish colonization, the American colonization, the destruction of Manila in World War II, and the eventual rehabilitation— told with humor, drama, candy, and carriage rides—it's clear no one can tell this story better.

Celdran founded Walk This Way in 2002. A performance artist by discipline, he envisioned a tour of Manila that bridged history and theater, the personal and the political. Philippine history is never more alive than on his tours, which sees him doing impressions of General Douglas McArthur and singing Big Band classics. "I always believe that art is the best way to change a nation," he says. "Inspiration over intimidation."

Why he's polarizing is another matter altogether. A longtime activist for HIV/AIDS awareness and reproductive health, Celdran staged a protest against the Church's opposition to the reproductive health bill in 2010. Dressed as Philippine national hero Jose Rizal, Celdran stormed the Manila Cathedral during mass carrying a sign that said "DAMASO" (a reference to the corrupt religious leader in Rizal's novel *Noli Me Tangere*), shouting "Stop getting involved in politics!" For his trouble, he was charged with "offending religious feelings" by the Catholic Bishops Conference of the Philippines and eventually sentenced to one year in prison.

"This is a setback for free speech in the Philippines, which prides itself on being a democracy," he said at the time. "This verdict should be reversed. Nobody should be jailed for voicing out an opinion or position, especially on a subject that concerns the lives of millions of Filipino women and mothers."

In a way, Celdran was merely echoing the actions national heroes have done in the past, the protagonists of his walking tours. And if his theatrical walking tours are not enough to serve as warning to Filipinos to avoid repeating mistakes of the past, he's willing to take his history lesson to the streets.

I always believe that art is the best way to change a nation. Inspiration over intimidation.

On his Walk This Way tours, Celdran meets the whole gamut of tourists—foreigners following the advice of the *New York Times*, balikbayans looking to learn about their country, locals who are tourists in their own country, eager for a refresher course on Philippine history.

The biggest misconception tourists have about Manila? "That there's no history here, and that it's soulless," he says.

"It's a reflection of you. If you can't find beauty and poetry in Manila, then you can't find beauty and poetry anywhere. You look at the city and either you reject it, or you accept it," he says. "That's it."

WRITTEN BY RAYMOND ANG
PHOTOGRAPHED BY CZAR KRISTOFF
SHOT ON LOCATION AT INTRAMUROS, MANILA

VISIT CARLOSCELDRANWALKS.WORDPRESS.COM
OR CELDRANTOURS.BLOGSPOT.COM FOR MORE DETAILS

NEIGHBORHOOD GUIDE:

Pasay

Beyond the Las Vegas-style entertainment complexes,
Pasay tells a larger story of Manila's history and heritage.

Pasay holds pockets of surprises that tell a larger story of Manila's history and heritage.

Don't let the gleaming Las Vegas-style entertainment complexes fool you. Pasay holds pockets of surprises that tell a larger story of Manila's history and heritage.

Accommodations

Start by checking in at The Henry Hotel (2680 F.B. Harrison St., Pasay; thehenryhotel.com), a series of interconnected 1950s-style Liberation houses— following cultural historian Fernando Zialcita's definition of the the postwar houses in the compound—that boast stately rooms, tall windows, and airy quarters. Though it's just a few blocks away from the busy byways of EDSA, here, the noise is left behind as soon as the gate closes, transporting you to a hidden sanctuary in the middle of the city. Though design hotels have a tendency to feel overly burdened with painstaking details, the Henry's charcoal gray houses are meant to look and feel like a home, recalling the balmy vibe of provincial summer retreats or colonial era manors with baldosa tiles, midcentury armoires, and polished clawfoot tubs.

Art and Design

Further down the acacia-lined driveway is the showroom of Eric Paras's A-11 (artellano11.ph). Paras is responsible for the interior design of the hotel, so the striking resemblance between the showroom and the hotel

A-11

PHOTOS BY JL JAVIER

interiors is gleefully intended. A peek into the three-house gallery of the interior designer's concept store is a reflection of his slow-living philosophy. The first house is the office with a bit of trinkets, ceramics, sculptures, and design items in store on the first floor—among them hybrid plates from Seletti, polished stone coasters, and space-themed tableware from Diesel. The second house is more attuned to home decor and accessories, strewn the way one might find them in an actual house. Works from contemporary artist also line the walls, allowing the space to resemble a gallery. The third house is more akin to a furniture storeroom, housing some pieces designed by Paras himself. When the actress Sarah Jessica Parker was in Manila, she visited A-11 and said that she could live there if she called Manila home.

Down by the front is veteran designer Joji Lloren's French

nouveau-style atelier. In case you're just dropping in for a visit (which means no time for an actual dress to be made), the fashion designer might be available for a quick chat. And just in front of A-11 is the Avellana Art Gallery, a two-story showcase of modern and folk art doubling as an exhibition space for contemporary artists. Run by Albert Avellana, the gallery was originally a storehouse for his art firm brokerage but has since evolved into a home for emerging Filipino artists who shy away from trends.

Outside the compound, there is Galleria Duemila (210 Loring St., Pasay; galleriaduemila.com). Founded in 1975, it remains the longest running gallery in the Philippines and boasts a collection of artwork from both Philippine masters and contemporary artists, from Fernando Amorsolo to Fernando Zobel.

Shopping

Shopping destinations include the markers in Cartimar (Cartimar Ave., Pasay) and Libertad (Antonio S. Arnaiz Ave., Pasay), which have assortments of fresh produce, Asian food items, and even pets. If you're in the mood for more commercial entertainment, at the end of EDSA is the Mall of Asia (Seaside Boulevard, Pasay; smmallofasia.com)—one of the biggest malls in Asia, a dream retail structure for SM Malls founder Henry Sy—and Blue Bay Walk (Cluster Bluebay Walk Building, corner EDSA, Diosdado Macapagal Blvd., Pasay; facebook.com/bluebaywalkofficial) which has fast food outlets and open spaces for biking, jogging, and walking.

— DON JAUCIAN

Eric Paras

Written by Don Jaucian
Photo by JL Javier

The interior designer behind A-11—the actress Sarah Jessica Parker's "home away from home" in Manila—might have found utopia in the heart of Pasay.

"This is what I dreamed of before," the interior designer Eric Paras says, about his small slice of nirvana that is the 2680 compound on F.B Harrison in Pasay. "It's like a utopia." On a languid day, the enclave is close to perfect, the noise of EDSA highway a far-off reminder that you're in one of the busiest places in the city. With the airport nearby, plus the sprawl of entertainment and commercial hubs dotting the reclaimed area near Manila Bay, his home—and workplace—is the ultimate retreat.

Paras first stumbled upon the post-war structure while doing business with a client and immediately fell in love with the place, having dreamed of living in a structure like this since his days as a college student walking by the Liberation-style houses along nearby Taft and Park Avenue. When one of the houses became vacant, Paras took the opportunity—not to live in at first, but to establish his concept store and design brand A-11. A few years later, when another house in the compound became available, Paras finally decided to move in and make it his home.

The imperfect character of old houses has always drawn Paras in, and his eccentric style has given his machuca-tiled home a lived-in feel that has grown organically: bottles from a pharmaceutical company act as flower vases, a taxidermied duck stands guard over a spacious library filled with secondhand bookstore finds, and chairs from an old hotel in Tokyo sit in the dining area, where Paras loves to serve home-cooked meals for friends and family. You get the impression that Paras almost never leaves the confines of his abode—it is his dream home, after all—but he also clearly enjoys what his neighborhood has to offer.

Grocery runs are done at the industrial S&R and the mall-like Cash and Carry nearby, where all sorts of reasonably priced imported goods—from chocolate to protein supplements—are sold alongside local products. A short bike ride away from the compound are two destination markets where fresh produce and organic food are available. "There's no frozen meat in the house because we buy it everyday," he shares.

Malate

Rich in culture and history, Malate has been in constant flux throughout the years.

Architectural Highlights

Malate has always been one of Manila's most vibrant districts. Rich in culture and history, the area has been in constant flux throughout the years. Interspersed within its streets are a mixture of styles, from classic to modern, haute and proletarian, and a slew of different transplanted cultures.

Restaurants

A trip down this corner of the city can lead you to Purple Yam (603 Julio Nakpil St. corner Bocobo Street; facebook.com/purpleyamph), a local branch of the established New York restaurant. Owner Amy Besa and her husband, chef Romy Dorotan, opened the Manila outpost in 2014 at Besa's old ancestral house, serving Pan Asian dishes that use locally grown produce. For more traditional colonial flavors, down the road sits Casa Armas (573 Julio Nakpil St.), which provides a glimpse of Spanish influence in the country, serving everything from tapas to platos principales paired with an impressive wine selection. While Malate is awash with Japanese restaurants, people often flock to Erra's Ramen (1755 Adriatico St.), an affordable ramen place that doubles as a watering hole. Don't let the plastic chairs fool you—the no-frills eatery may be simple, but customers line up just to get a table here. If the comfort of soup doesn't appeal to you, head over to Aristocrat (432 San Andres St. corner Roxas Blvd.; aristocrat.com.ph). This Malate institution offers a complete selection of Filipino dishes, but the dish that built its reputation—

The Ramon Magsaysay Center

This seemingly flimsy construction was designed by A.J. Luz Associates together with designer Pietro Belluschi and Alfred Yee Associates. Built in 1967, the structure has withstood pretty much everything nature sent its way, from the constant typhoons that hit Manila to 7.8-magnitude earthquakes, all thanks to its then-novel structural system that resembles a tree—a main column in the middle of the building supported by secondary pillars that help it move with natural forces rather than against them.

De La Salle Most Blessed Sacrament Chapel

Designed by Tomas Mapua, the chapel was built in the 1930s. During the war, it served as a refuge for its occupants, the Brothers of the Christian Schools, together with a group of nearby survivors. Its place in history is cemented as the site of the 1945 massacre, where a group of 20 Japanese soldiers took the lives of more than 70 refugees inside the chapel—which has left bloodstains on its walls to this day. The chapel now serves as an important site for the Brothers and also houses a relic of St. John Baptist de La Salle.

barbecue chicken with peanut sauce served with java rice and pickled papaya—remains the crowd favorite here.

For specialty coffee, head on to Blocleaf Café (Hop-Inn Hotel, 1850 M.H. Del Pilar St.; facebook.com/blocleafcafe)—a well-designed Japanese-style neighborhood haunt. Try their mocha made with local tablea and seasonal cakes such as the delighful ube cheesecake.

A welcome addition to the neighborhood, The Shipyard (Bocobo St. corner Malvar St., Malate) is a two-story structure composed of shipping containers serving fried chicken, Filipino street food, burgers, and kebabs.

Night Life

Malate nightlife is just as varied as its dining scene, and offers all forms of entertainment. Bars line the streets and most of them, such as The Other Office Piano Bar & Restaurant (1122 Mabini St. U.N. Ave.), carry fascinating histories. With its old-fashioned interiors and live musical performances, the bar has served as "another office" to newsmen and politicians in the past. Similarly, Oarhouse (1688-B Bocobo St.; facebook.com/oarhousepub), with its bohemian decor, was a favorite meeting place of journalists and photographers in its heyday. While

The Artist's Haunts

Munchen Grill Pub	The Other Office	Cowboy Grill
1316 A. Mabini St., Ermita	1122 A. Mabini St., Ermita	11910 Mabini St. cor. Arquiza St., Ermita

Interspersed within its streets are a mixture of styles, from classic to modern, haute and proletarian, and a slew of different transplanted cultures.

both bars had a specific clientele in the past, the appreciation for these unobtrusive watering holes has carried over to the younger generation, thanks to both establishments' winning bar room philosophy of serving good food and superior drinks. For those looking for a more interactive experience, a trip to The Library (1739 Ma. Orosa St.; thelibrary.com.ph) will not disappoint. This gay comedy bar and restaurant features some of the best performances in town, ranging from routines and skits to musical performances, some of which require audience participation. While not a bar per se, the Syquia Apartments (1991 M.H. Del Pilar St.)

is home almost exclusively to artists living as a tight-knit community in the Art Deco building known for its extremely long waitlist. While its colorful pool of residents are known for throwing the best parties this side of Manila, an invitation from a tenant must be secured before one is allowed admission.

Art and Culture

Even if revelry isn't your thing, Malate still has much to offer. From sins to virtues, the first stop would obviously be the Malate Church (2000 M.H. Del Pilar Street). A mixture of Muslim and Baroque architecture, the church was established more than two centuries ago, making it one of the oldest—if not the oldest—landmark in Malate. The district is also home to Bangko Sentral ng Pilipinas, which supports two museums that reside within its compound. The Money Museum (A. Mabini St. cor. P. Ocampo St.) walks visitors through the different stages and evolution of monetary items found in the Philippines from the pre-Hispanic period to present. The Metropolitan Museum of Manila (A. Mabini corner P. Ocampo; metmuseum.ph) on the other hand houses contemporary art by both Filipinos and international artists. For more prominent sites, drop by The Ramon Magsaysay Center (1680 Roxas Boulevard; rmaft.org.ph). While its design may appear to defy natural laws, it is now considered ahead of its time for using pre-cast and pre-stressed concrete beams to achieve its unique look. Additionally, Malate also houses De La Salle University, home of The Most Blessed Sacrament (La Salle Building, 2401 Taft Avenue), an Art Deco chapel designed by Tomas Mapua.

THE SHIPYARD

PHOTO BY KAI HUANG

— MIGUEL ORTEGA

Maria Taniguchi

Written by Mara Coson
Photo by JL Javier

The internationally-awarded artist—the winner of Hugo Boss Asia Art 2015—talks about the neighborhood that's seen her grow up.

Up the thick narra stairs of the North Syquia apartments, or up its old elevator, possibly the first passenger elevator in the Philippines, is the artist Maria Taniguchi's studio. The large, high-ceilinged apartment opens up to big windows and plenty of sunlight. Charlie the dog basks in the sun atop a wooden stepladder. Devil's vines hang from the balcony and leaves of a potted selloum looks out onto the street.

Taniguchi studied at the Philippine High School for the Arts in Mount Makiling, and each weekend the bus would drop its students off at the Cultural Center of the Philippines, mere minutes away from Malate. Up until college she has had memories of dinner at Patio Guernica or Munchen Grill and Pub with her uncle and aunt. "*Guernica*, the painting, was made in 1937, around the same time as North Syquia," Taniguchi notes. "Less than 10 years after Guernica was bombed, Manila suffered the devastation of the Second World War, leveling most of the pre-war architecture except a few, including North Syquia."

North Syquia, one of the few Art Deco buildings to remain, along with its sister building South Syquia located two doors down, are well known for the range of interesting personalities who over the last few decades have called its apartments home—artists, playwrights, designers, musicians, photographers—and with them, the infamously wild parties they threw when the sun set over Manila Bay.

A quiet tenant, Taniguchi finds in the stout, stable North Syquia a perfect setting for work. Here, Taniguchi's brick paintings are laid out on saw horses, catching the bright morning light—an ideal time to paint each and every brick onto her canvas. "I need a lot of light for the paintings. The paintings are really dark, so I like that in the morning I get to see the work in natural lighting, and it's completely different when I work at night with the lights on, which flattens the surface of the paintings."

"Another thing is that this house is really good for reading," she says. "I spend a lot of time at a desk by my favorite window that looks out to an abandoned deck area that's now grown over by rosal and bougainvillea. The ideal is for a space to be as much a thinking space as it is a doing space."

LEARN FROM A LOCAL:
Pepe Diokno

Pepe Diokno was just 22 years old when he won the Lion of the Future Award at the 2009 Venice Film Festival for *Engkwentro* (2009), his first film—which he completed while still an undergrad at the University of the Philippines.

And he's not the only filmmaker making international news. In the last few years, the triumph of Philippine independent cinema can be felt in its presence in international film festivals and its newfound ability to cross over to local mainstream audiences and box-office success. Veteran filmmakers like Lav Diaz (winner of the 2016 Venice Film Festival's Golden Lion) and Brilliant Mendoza (who won Best Director at the 62nd Cannes Film Festival) have become fixtures on the international film fest circuit, winning some of world cinema's most prestigious awards.

"What I've found in the age of globalization, at least with films, is that the more local a movie is, the more global it becomes," Diokno says. "In my travels, I've met a lot of people who are so passionate about our movies that it surprises me. What these people know— and what I want more people to know—is how rich the buffet of our cinema is. That ours is one of the oldest film industries in the world, and that the variety of films that we make is amazing, from rom-coms to arthouse movies."

In the Philippines, the stories we tell are very specific. Our country is fertile ground for material.

A newspaper columnist since his teens, Diokno has always been keenly aware of the power of storytelling, and the responsibility that power comes with.

"In the Philippines, the stories we tell are very specific. Our country is fertile ground for material," he says. "This is a country where the super rich live side-by-side with the poor and where western colonial influences mate with Asian culture. Even our national identity is conflicted—we're a collection of tribes, each with different a language and way of life. How can you not find inspiration in all of that?"

WRITTEN BY RAYMOND ANG
PHOTOGRAPHED BY JOSEPH PASCUAL
SHOT ON LOCATION ACROSS THE MANILA CENTRAL POST OFFICE, LIWASANG
BONIFACIO, MANILA

The Director's Picks

Five films that will tell you about the Philippines, according to Pepe Diokno.

"For a sense of the past, Lav Diaz's *Hele Sa Hiwagang Hapis* (2016)," he says, beginning his list with the internationally-acclaimed Diaz's eight-hour epic on Philippine history and mythology. A Berlinale Silver Bear winner, Meryl Streep hailed Diaz a genius after watching *Hele*. "He rearranged the molecules of my brain." Diokno's independent feature film company Epicmedia produced *Hele*.

Next, Diokno lists two classics of Philippine cinema. "To learn about the nightmare we're still trying to shake off, Lino Brocka's *Maynila Sa Mga Kuko ng Liwanag* (1975). To understand how Filipinos can laugh through [anything], Joey Gosiengfiao's *Temptation Island* (1980)." For an understanding of the current political and social climate, he includes two of his own films. "For our current nightmare, my film *Engkwentro* (2009). And for my take on what Filipino culture is, my film *Kapatiran* (2015)."

PART

3

and More

The best way to misjudge a country is to regard it by the two places it is best known for: its capital and its most popular tourist destination.

WRITTEN BY ARIANNA LIM AND ANDREA ANG

A Country on Your Tongue

One of the country's culinary heroes—Asia's Best Female Chef 2016—on why regionality might be how Filipino food, long dubbed the international scene's next It cuisine, finally takes over the world.

BY MARGARITA FORÉS

They always ask about the adobo. It is, after all, the most iconic dish we have.

ADOBO 101?

FOR A PRIMER ON PHILIPPINE CUISINE GO TO PAGE 18

At the trade fairs, festivals, and gastronomic congresses I've been to around the world, I've always found that people are generally open to Filipino cuisine. They have their perceptions, of course, that our cuisine can be summed up in the "weird" balut, or that it ends and begins with the pancit, lumpia, and adobo. There's so much more to Filipino food than that.

The regionality of Filipino cuisine is one aspect that is only getting some attention now. It's an aspect that reveals a lot about who we are. They might know adobo, for example, as our national dish, but it comes differently depending on which part of the Philippines you're in. The adobo in Batangas has a yellow hue because it's cooked with ginger; red among the Ilonggos as annatto seeds are used; and crisp-fried in other parts of the Visayas as the meat is slow-cooked in lard.

The food in Central Luzon—Pampanga, Bulacan, and Tarlac—is so different from the food in Metro Manila, even though it's just a few hours away. The cuisine there is insular, more inward. They eat crickets and rice birds; they have river prawns that are not from the coast; and they have a lot of sticky rice because a strong Spanish influence affected most of Luzon. At the same time, if you go to Visayas, you have a lot of seafood, shellfish, and dishes that lean more on the sweet side as the land grows sugarcanes.

And then, all of a sudden, there's this whole new frontier in Mindanao that the local food industry is so excited about because a lot of us in Manila are only discovering it now. The cuisine in the far south is so different from the rest of the country because it's the least affected by colonization. That's why their food is closest to that of Malaysia's and Indonesia's. Their dishes are layered in flavor.

PHOTO BY MARK NICDAO

They always ask about the adobo. It is, after all, the most iconic dish we have.

It's like the fare in Thailand, Malaysia, and Indonesia—they have condiments that are made with pureed chili and smoked coconut, and a certain variety of onion that only grows in their area. They sauté those ingredients and turn it into a paste called palapa, which they mix into or eat with their dishes. They even have things like rendang or satay, and items that appear more Indonesian and Malaysian than Filipino. But actually, that's the cuisine we had even before the Spaniards or the Chinese came to trade with us.

And so, with an international audience that's suddenly so open to our cuisine, it becomes very important to have an awareness of what we decide to present to them. What has become my advocacy is presenting the great quality of our produce.

At international fairs, we usually highlight things like our cacao, coffee, heirloom rice, and sweet mangoes. Of

course, they expect to try our adobo. And because that dish is usually our point of entry, what I try to do is use that to introduce them to other aspects of our cuisine—serve the adobo with our heirloom rice, and an atchara (local pickled vegetables; traditionally, grated unripe papaya) using whatever vegetables we find. I explain to them how they have to have pair the adobo with atchara to cut through the richness and the saltiness of the dish. From there, I introduce them to the idea of how sourness is probably the most prominent flavor profile in our cuisine, and how this is a function of our climate—we need the sourness to preserve our food because our country is very warm.

Our cuisine is about balancing the flavors. Our soups are usually sour and so we try to counteract it with something salty. If you have a rich stew that is very Malay, like our kare-kare, it has a tendency to be bland, so we add shrimp paste to counteract that. Through our local produce, we are able to explain the philosophy behind the cuisine. That is an awareness that has to be communicated when we're explaining Filipino cuisine to a foreigner who's trying our food for the first time.

> They might know adobo, for example, as our national dish, but it comes differently depending on which part of the Philippines you're in.

When I got back from my studies in Italy in 1986, the biggest challenge for me was finding the right kind of tomato for my dishes. Back then, we didn't have much of that in the Philippines. At first, I saw that as a challenge. Later, it became an opportunity. I had to learn how to work with our local tomatoes to see how I can process them and work with them so that they could come close to the flavor I was looking for. Adapting the recipe to our produce helped me find my own way of understanding what we could do with what we have, and how that could relate to what the rest of the world was doing.

For example, thinking about the iconic Italian dishes I enjoyed, like prosciutto with melon or prosciutto with figs, I started to think about what I could do with our produce in mind. A fresh fig has a certain grittiness, and when it's sweet, it's sweet. Then I thought, what if I paired the prosciutto with our beautiful chico? That actually came out better than the fig.

At the same time, I grew up eating queso de bola with guava jelly and bananas with my grandmother. In Italy, when I would eat in restaurants, they would always end the meal with a cheese course, and they would pair the Italian cheeses with honey or marmelatas. I said to myself, "If I could pair Parmesan with the beautiful jelly you get in Negros, that would be so cool."

I don't like the word "fusion." I think what I do is executing Italian food in its truest sense using Filipino ingredients.

Instead of just paying an homage to Italian cuisine, it ends up elevating Filipino ingredients—because it's so good, and when you use it side by side with what the rest of the world has to offer, and then putting together these so-called world-class dishes, you show the rest of the world that what we have can stand beside them.

I think the most important lesson I learned from Italy is the way they respect their ingredients, how many centuries of culture has become the base for all their produce. Whoever makes balsamico today is still the family that has been making it for centuries, still using the same process. It's the same thing with cheese makers, and the guys who make prosciutto—the integrity of their products is absolutely their power.

Applying that to the Philippines, we also have our iconic ingredients—bangus from Bonuan, mangoes from Guimaras, salt from Ilocos, calamansi from Mindoro, sugar from Negros. All these things can actually be certified as "the best." That's what got me started wanting to go around and discovering other local products.

Recently, I realized that maybe we're lucky we didn't get industrialized. That has been seen as a weakness for us but in a way, because we're so backward, we're actually at the forefront of what's happening right now. Everybody in the world is trying to go back to old ways of planting, trying to go back to the more primitive and cleaner way of growing things. And that's what we can boast of. We're still doing it the old-fashioned way. We don't have to undo so much. In that sense, we're way ahead of mostly everyone else.

As told to Raymond Ang

Margarita Forés is a Filipino chef best known for her background in Italian cuisine, and constant exploration of Filipino produce and flavors. Her expertise in the field have allowed her to collaborate with the likes of Vicky Cheng and Hiroyasu Kawate.

115

7 Trips to Take Outside Manila

The best way to misjudge a country is to regard it by the two places it's best known for: its capital, and its most popular tourist destination.

The capital of the Philippines, it must be said, is easily misunderstood. Manila's chaos and confusion tend to obscure its thriving creative capital, through which bold contemporary art galleries and a lively indie music scene coexist alongside the ultra-urbanized neighborhoods' penchant for speakeasies and third wave coffee. Far removed from the Old Manila of Spanish and Chinese influence, the brave new world of skyscrapers and shopping malls rubs shoulders with sprawling shantytowns. It's this patchwork of culture and history that allows the capital to hold its own among its Southeast Asian neighbors—but it's also what has turned Manila into its own beast, a would-be self-contained system that has always marched a little out of step with the rest of the Philippines.

The title of top tourist draw arguably belongs to Boracay, a tiny island in Visayas famous for its immaculate white sand and 24/7 party culture. A few decades ago, its spartan creature comforts and long stretches of talcum-like sand kept it a paradise among locals and free-spirited backpackers. Today it is as notorious for its cluster of partygoers, as it is famous for its white sand and azure waters. Its frenetic energy is both keeping it alive and driving its downward spiral. On its famed White Beach, tranquility is best found in the early mornings, when last night's partygoers are in recovery. Not unlike Manila, Boracay has evolved into its own freewheeling entity, its beauty now a backdrop for more resorts, bars, and people than the island can handle.

It's important, then, to look beyond Manila and Boracay when you're planning a trip to the Philippines. In doing so, travelers will find sights and traditions as diffused and multifarious as our seven thousand islands: mountains that summit above the clouds, miles of powder-fine beaches, and peoples decidedly removed from the ways and means of the metropolis. While you'd be hard pressed to see it all, a select few daytrips and weekend excursions allow for a glimpse of what the rest of the country can offer when you're ready to head back out for more.

—ARIANNA LIM

Tanay

Home to an assortment of easily-accessible rivers,
waterfalls, and hiking trails, Tanay is your best bet for
escaping the city without traveling too far.

The municipality of Tanay sits 60 kilometers east of Manila. Bounded by portions of the Sierra Madre mountain range, it's home to an assortment of easily-accessible rivers, waterfalls, and hiking trails that make it your best bet for leaving the city behind without having to travel too far.

The Itinerary

How To Get There

Head out first thing in the morning and drive—or, for the more adventurous, bike—to Barangay Daraitan. A former logging site, the area is now a popular ecotourism destination that boasts of natural pools, caves, and a short hike through its namesake mountain.

Make your primary destination the Tinipak River, where clear, cool water rushes past massive limestone formations.

If clambering over the boulders or going spelunking through the adjacent cave don't complete your itinerary already, make them the reward for completing the traverse of the neighboring Mt. Daraitan—a steep but fairly straightforward ascent with views of Laguna de Bay and the surrounding Sierra Madre mountains.

The nearby Masungi Georeserve (Garden Cottages, Kilometer 47, Marcos Highway, Baras, Rizal; masungigeoreserve.com), though not technically in Tanay, is also a popular alternative for those looking for an outdoor adventure with slightly more structure. The conservation area allows you a close view of karst terrain, with a distinct trail that features a hanging bridge, rope courses, and limestone peaks and cave formations. Due to its popularity, it's best to make reservations here well in advance.

From the transport terminal in StarMall Mandaluyong, catch a commuter van or jeepney heading to Tanay Public Market.

From there, flag a tricycle to take you to your desired destination.

If Masungi Georeserve is your first stop, its location makes going by private vehicle a simpler choice.

To travel via public transportation, take a commuter van or jeepney from Cubao to Cogeo Gate 2, then catch another jeep heading to Sampaloc, Tanay and get off at Garden Cottages

DAY TRIP:

Antipolo City

With the rise of a must-see art gallery and a thriving food scene, Antipolo is fast becoming a choice destination for weekend day trips.

Though situated just a stone's throw away from Manila, Antipolo has managed to keep the worst of the metropolis' commotion at bay. For years it was known best among religious circles as a pilgrimage site, where devotees made regular trips to the Marian image of Our Lady of Peace and Good Voyage in the Antipolo Cathedral. Of late, however, it's welcomed a broader set of visitors drawn in by the presence of a favored art gallery and good food that won't break the bank.

The Itinerary

A 1.3-hectare space dedicated to the exhibition of local contemporary art, the Pinto Art Museum (1 Sierra Madre St., Grand Heights Subdivision) is now the go-to destination and Instagram hotspot of Antipolo. Situated in the Silangan Gardens and designed by artist Antonio Leaño, the museum originally housed the private collection of neurologist and art enthusiast Dr. Joven Cuanang until he opened its doors to the public in 2010.

Exploring the museum's six galleries could be a full-day itinerary in itself, but if you'd like to refuel before heading back to Manila, consider a stop at Marison's (2/F Vista Mall Antipolo and U/G Robinsons Place Antipolo, Sumulong Highway; marisonsph.com) for local fare, or Vieux Chalet (Taktak Road, Antipolo City; vieuxchaletswissrestaurant.com) for a hearty Swiss meal and a bird's-eye-view of the city.

How To Get There

Take your pick of starting points from Cubao Farmer's Market, StarMall Mandaluyong, SM Megamall, or Robinsons Galleria.

Catch a jeepney or commuter van heading to Antipolo and get off either at Ynares Center or Antipolo Church.

From there, hire a tricycle to take you to your desired destination.

VIEUX CHALET'S SHRIMP COCKTAIL

VIEUX CHALET'S MANGO STICKY RICE

MARISON'S PORK BINAGONG

MARISON'S KARE KARE

MARISON'S SANSRIVAL

DAY TRIP:

Tagaytay City

The easiest, closest, and least rough-and-tumble getaway from both Manila's cramped malls and the oppressiveness of its heat, Tagaytay is a sweet escape that still delivers.

Recent years have seen Tagaytay transformed from a favorite weekend getaway to a near-extension of Metro Manila, replete with foreign franchises and slow-moving traffic. Yet its appeal has remained stubbornly intact. It's at once the easiest, closest, and least rough-and-tumble escape from both the tedium of Manila's cramped malls and the oppressiveness of its heat. So long as you travel outside of rush hour, Tagaytay—with its homegrown restaurants that trump fast food giants and its overlooking views of Taal Lake—still delivers.

The Itinerary

How To Get There

Making the trip to Tagaytay for a meal at one of chef Tony Boy Escalante's three restaurants (antoniosrestaurant.ph) is always a good idea.

If your time, budget, and appetite restrict you to just one, make it Antonio's (Purok 138, Brgy. Neogan, Luksuhin-Mangas Rd.; +63917 899 2866), recognized by the Miele Guide and Asia's 50 Best Restaurants for excellent food and gracious service that never leaves you wanting.

Breakfast at Antonio's (Aguinaldo Highway, Brgy. Bagong Tubig) is its more relaxed younger brother, offering an all-day breakfast menu that keeps things casual without conceding the brand's trademark attention to detail.

But if you'd prefer to explore Filipino cuisine, order family style at Balay Dako (Tagaytay-Nagsugbu Highway) or head in first thing on a weekend morning to get a seat at their breakfast buffet.

Because Tagaytay is best visited with a loose agenda and a careless schedule, you wouldn't be faulted for heading back home after a good meal and a few hours of conversation. But if you'd like to make the most of your trip, cap it off with cocktails and a massage at QiWellness Living (Aguinaldo Highway, Brgy. Maharlika East; qiwellnessliving.ph).

From Uniwide Coastal Mall, EGI Mall near the LRT Gil Puyat Station, or StarMall Mandaluyong, take a bus or commuter van bound for Batangas via Tagaytay.

Once you reach Tagaytay, get off at the Tagaytay Rotunda and get around via jeepney or tricycle.

BREAKFAST AT ANTONIO'S CORNED BEEF

BALAY DAKO'S BULALO NA BAKA

BREAKFAST AT ANTONIO'S PANCAKES

ANTONIO'S ROASTED BONE MARROW

ANTONIO'S LECHON DE LECHE

LONG WEEKEND (3-4 DAYS):

Siargao

Once a sleepy locale frequented more by dedicated surfers than your average beach bums, this small island off the coast of Surigao del Norte is fast becoming a preferred tropical paradise.

A small island off the coast of Surigao del Norte in Mindanao, Siargao was once a sleepy locale frequented more by dedicated surfers than your average beach bums. But the latter have finally caught on, pulled in by the island's long stretches of fine white sand, secluded lagoons, and sprawling mangrove forests. This newfound attention is well deserved, though the right balance between virgin island pleasures and new creature comforts must always be kept in mind.

The Itinerary

Whether you're an expert or can barely keep upright, getting on a surfboard is a must in Siargao. As the country's rightful surfing capital, waves here are available nearly year-round and can reach seven feet or higher at peak season.

Take your pick from the 15 surf breaks—the most famous among them being Cloud Nine, owing to its thick, barreling waves—or else try your hand at windsurfing and kitesurfing.

For a break from the adrenaline, take your snorkeling gear to Magpupungko beach, where underwater rock formations separate calm and clear tidal pools from the crashing waves of the Pacific.

If you can tear yourself away from the waterfront, get a ride to the town of Del Carmen and hire a boat to take you through its dense mangrove forests. Spanning an impressive 4,000 hectares, this reserve is home to rare and endangered plant and wildlife, as well as the remote Sugba lagoon, where turquoise waters and high surrounding hills offer a quiet respite from the busy beaches.

To venture farther out, book an island hopping tour and see the nearby Naked, Dako, and Gayum islands.

How To Get There

From Manila, the best option is to take a flight via Skyjet, which flies straight to Siargao.

When you land in Sayak Airport, you can reach General Luna (a 45 – 60 minute drive away) by van or motorbike, both of which can be hailed outside the airport.

LONG WEEKEND (3-4 DAYS):

Palawan

The draw of Philippine tourism is
built largely on our beaches, and
Palawan stands chief among them.

Palawan should need no introduction. The draw of Philippine tourism is built largely on our beaches, and Palawan stands chief among them. The country's westernmost island, it's home to powder-fine white sand beaches, towering limestone cliffs, and the Tubbataha reserve and its 10,000 hectares of coral reef—to name just a few highlights. A favorite destination among Filipinos and foreigners alike, Palawan's prestige will live on after every party beach has reached its logical conclusion.

The Itinerary

If you opt to stay within Puerto Princesa, the province's main point of entry, set aside a day to explore the 22,000-hectare Subterranean River National Park. A UNESCO World Heritage Site, its highlight is an underground river that runs for some eight kilometers and features stellar cave chambers that rise to over 60 meters.

Once it's been checked off your list of must-sees, take your pick of the nearby beaches, including Nagtabon, Napsan, and Talaudyong, or make trips to the waterfalls of Olongoan and Salakot.

If you're around from April to October, try your luck at sighting the spinner dolphins that play just off Puerto Princesa Bay.

Those who can be convinced to stay inland can grab a couple of craft beers at the Palawano Brewery (82 Manalo St, Puerto Princesa; palawenobrewery. com), or support local culture and alternative livelihoods through Rurungan Sa Tubod Foundation (The Rurungan Compound, Abanico Road, Puerto Princesa; rurungan.org), which offers beautiful piña textiles woven by women from the surrounding communities. There is of course much more to see outside Puerto Princesa, the most popular destinations being the islands of El Nido and Coron, known for towering limestone cliffs, pristine lagoons, hot springs, and seawater so clear you can see to the floor.

As a bonus, if your budget and schedule permit, a diving trip in Tubbataha Reefs Natural Park— situated at the heart of the Coral Triangle and home to 600 species of fish, 360 species of corals, 11 species of sharks, and 13 species of dolphins and whales—is not an opportunity to be missed. Get on a liveaboard boat and see for yourself how the Philippines earned its title as the global center of marine biodiversity.

How To Get There

Take a direct flight from Manila to Puerto Princesa via Philippine Airlines, Air Asia, or Cebu Pacific, then get a tricycle to take you where you need to go.

To get to El Nido, you can either take the six-hour land transfer from Puerto Princesa via the Cherry Bus or Roro Bus lines, or, if you're not pressed for budget, charter a flight from Manila.

Getting to Coron is simpler, with direct flights via Philippine Airlines and Cebu Pacific to Busuanga, to be followed by a 40-minute shuttle van ride to Coron town.

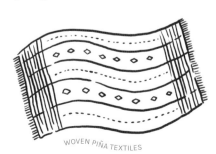

WOVEN PIÑA TEXTILES

TUBBATAHA REEFS NATURAL PARK

Ifugao

Famous for its man-made rice terraces, a visit
to Ifugao is an excellent way to escape the
city's hyperconnectivity.

Venturing into Ifugao, a landlocked province in the Cordilleras, is a different sort of adventure. The travel is arduous, the creature comforts minimal, and the range of activities arguably sparse—but given the right mindset, it can offer a more promising trip than any beach or city can. The region is famous for its man-made rice terraces, a demonstration of the sustainable ecological knowledge and cultural traditions of generations of small-scale farmers. Apart from offering scenic photo ops, a visit to Ifugao is an excellent way to escape the city's hyperconnectivity, reflect on man's reliance on nature, and take a hard look at tourism's implications on development.

How To Get There

Sleep off the nine-hour drive by getting a seat on the evening buses of Ohayami Transit.

Upon arrival in Banaue, take a jeepney to the Batad Saddle, the closest point to Batad village that a vehicle can go.

From there, it's a 40-minute trek to the village. If you're a group of 15 or so people, it becomes more convenient and cost-efficient to rent the entire jeepney for yourselves.

The Itinerary

Ifugao is home to five different UNESCO-listed rice terrace clusters, but the amphitheater-like structure of Batad makes it the crowd favorite.

To get there, take an overnight bus ride to Banaue, then find a jeepney to take you to the town. Make the most of your travel time and the fresh mountain air by riding topload on the vehicle's roof, foregoing what would otherwise be a dull, bumpy drive. So long as you watch for low-hanging wires and abrupt turns, it's guaranteed to be a worthwhile ride. Once in Batad, enjoy the peace of being forcibly disconnected from any cell service or internet connection as you walk along the mud and stone borders of the rice terraces. Each of these leveled ponds has been carefully carved to follow the contours of the mountains, creating an ingenious system of sustainable irrigation. Visit in April through May or October through November, when the crops transform each terrace into a vibrant sea of green.

For a challenge, take a side trip to the Tappiyah Falls, a relatively tough but scenic trek that involves steep descending steps. Cool down in the waterfall's chilly pool before making your way back up again. Whatever the particulars of your itinerary, treat the locals as the rightful stars of the show. You'll be there as a paying customer, but keep in mind that you're being granted permission to enjoy what has taken them generations of hard labor to build and maintain.

TAPPIYAH FALLS

LONG WEEKEND (4 DAYS):

Ilocos Norte

Lining the northwest coast of Luzon, Ilocos Norte, hosts centuries-old religious structures, picturesque if chilly beaches, and of course, signature Ilocano cuisine.

Though the Ilocos Region is best known for the historic colonial city of Vigan in Ilocos Sur, the argument can be made that there's far more to see in its sibling province up north. Lining the northwest coast of Luzon, Ilocos Norte, apart from being the hometown of late dictator Ferdinand Marcos, hosts centuries-old religious structures, picturesque if chilly beaches, and of course, signature Ilocano cuisine.

How To Get There

The simplest way is to fly to Laoag, Ilocos Norte via Cebu Pacific or Philippine Airlines, then take a tricycle or jeep to the city proper.

You may also opt to take a 12-hours bus trip via Partas or Florida Bus from Cubao.

With either option, it's best to rent a private vehicle to be able to hit all your desired destinations.

The alternative is making the long drive in a private vehicle. This may make for a more tiring trip, but you'll own your time rather than working around public transportation schedules.

The Itinerary

Hitting Ilocos Norte requires a lot of land travel, so indulge in a comfortable home base. Book a house in Sitio Remedios (Brgy. Victoria, Currimao; sitioremediosilocosnorte. com), a "heritage village resort" whose villas pay homage to midcentury Ilocano residences with materials salvaged from various Ilocos Norte towns. Then pay a visit to the 300-year-old Paoay Church, whose localized style of Baroque architecture earned it a spot on the UNESCO World Heritage list. Stop by the workshop of National Living Treasure Magdalena Gamayo, the master textile weaver who, now well into her 90s, continues to wield careful control over her intricate inabel patterns.

For the more adventurous, scramble across the massive limestones of the Kapurpurawan Rock Formation, or head to the coastal desert of La Paz and ride down the dunes on a sandboard or a 4x4. Finally, wrap up with a walk among the towering windmills that line the nine-kilometer shoreline of Bagui Bay, best done at sunset.

Whether you tick all of these off your list or choose to your liking, do it between thorough taste tests of Ilocano food, from the simple but flavorful vegetables of poqui-poqui to the heart-stopping deep fried crispy pork belly of bagnet.

The Art Pilgrimage

Manila's art scene continues to thrive thanks to globally competitive contemporary art galleries, museums, and private collections made available to the public, such as Pinto Art Gallery. That momentum isn't exclusive to the city. Here are three more destinations worth taking an art pilgrimage to.

Las Casas Filipinas de Acuzar

The country's first and only heritage site by the sea brings together architectural pieces from different eras and parts of the country, and then reconstructs them plank by plank. The space also hosts the experimentation and collaborations funded by Bellas Artes Projects, a non-profit foundation supporting the production of contemporary artists. *Brgy. Ibaba, Bagac, Bataan www.lascasasfilipinas.com*

BenCab Museum

Awarded the National Artist of the Philippines for Visual Arts in 2006, BenCab has long been hailed as a master of contemporary Philippine art. For a thorough survey of his formidable body of work, you can't do better than his own BenCab Museum, which he established in 2009 in Baguio City, one of the country's top summer destinations. *Km. 6 Asin Road, Tadiangan, Tuba, Benguet, Philippines www.bencabmuseum.org*

Fundacion Pacita

Once the studio home of the internationally acclaimed artist Pacita Abad, Fundacion Pacita in Batanes is a hotel that pays homage to the artist and its roots, with Ivatan-inspired rooms and suites. Each uniquely designed room is adorned by art from both well-known and up-and-coming artists. Of course, the real draw is Batanes itself—the pure, unadulterated beauty of which you can experience in at the comfort of the hotel. *Brgy. Chanarian, Tukon Basco, Batanes www.fundacionpacita.ph*

The Golden Ticket

The Philippines' generous smattering of sparkling beaches have long become a draw for tourists all over the world. But apart from providing all the requisites for an upscale home away from home—private butlers, sleek interiors, utmost privacy, bespoke itineraries—these high-end resorts excel in the intangible.

DEDON ISLAND   PHOTO BY TOTO LABRADOR

Dedon Island

Located 45 minutes from Cebu, Siargao has gained traction for its picturesque tidal pools, island hopping opportunities, and yet-to-be-rivaled year-round surfing scene. This boutique resort offers a range of activities on and off the beach to cater to every guest, from water sports and surfing lessons to island excursions and even cooking lessons—all in an impeccably designed paradise filled with Dedon furniture.

How to Get There: Daily flights from Cebu International Airport to Sayak Domestic Airport on Siargao, followed by a 30-minute journey from the airport to the resort in Dedon's signature jeepney. Alternatively, the staff can arrange for a private charter/helicopter for your entire journey.

Amanpulo

Famed for its collection of award-winning resorts across the world, the Aman brand's Amanpulo, located on Pamalican Island, is arguably the Philippines' most prestigious and exclusive travel destination. While each casita—along with the personalized service, luxurious amenities, and unparalleled privacy that come with it—can cost quite a pretty penny, those who frequent Amanpulo, among them local society's upper crust as well as international celebrities who appreciate being able to come and go undetected, find the hefty price tag well worth the splurge.

How to Get There: Direct flights from Amanpulo's own airstrip in Manila take 70 minutes of travel time.

aman.com/resorts/amanpulo

AMANPULO

Pangulasian Island

Located in Bacuit Bay in Palawan, this is the most luxurious property in the El Nido Resorts portfolio. With only 42 villas set on powdery white sand and surrounded by tropical forest, Pangulasian puts an emphasis on eco-luxury by practicing sustainable hospitality and promoting marine wildlife.

How to Get There: Daily flights from Airswift, Manila Domestic Airport Terminal 4, followed by a five-minute ride to El Nido Town Pier by land and 30- to 45-minute boat ride to Pangulasian.

elnidoresorts.com/pangulasian-island

DEDON ISLAND   PHOTO BY TOTO LABRADOR

BALESIN

PHOTOS BY PATRICK MARTIRES

COURTESY OF AMANPULO

Balesin Island

Alphaland Corporation's private getaway is set on 500 hectares of land punctuated by over seven kilometers of white sand beaches. Featuring seven themed villages inspired by some of the world's most renowned beach destinations such as St. Tropez, Mykonos, Phuket, and Toscana, Balesin boasts superb F&B offerings and a long list of activities to keep families fully occupied, from horseback riding to indoor and outdoor sports. The catch? Balesin is a members-only destination, and even with sponsorship, guests must be accompanied by the member.

How to Get There: A 20-minute flight from Manila on Balesin's fleet of private jets.

balesinisland.com

ARANAZ, GREENBELT 5, MAKATI CITY

The Pasalubong Guide

Pasalubong: In English, "(Something) for when you welcome me."

It's hard to pin down, exactly, why Filipinos care so much about the *pasalubong*, the tradition of buying something from a trip abroad or out of town to bring home to loved ones. Maybe it's because the communities are tight-knit. Maybe it's because it's always Christmas here. Or maybe it's because there's nothing more exciting than coming home.

In the last few decades, Manila has swayed toward American mall culture—franchise shopping, fluorescent-lit department stores, and fast fashion, all encased within behemoth commercial centers whose numbered buildings blur in memory. But in recent years, the retail scene has changed for the better. Manila shopping no longer feels generic, no longer a melting pot of exports from the U.S. or neighboring Asian countries. Now accessible in ways they never were before—in no small part thanks to the Internet—there is finally a distinct sense of what is ours.

Our clothes now come from within the original minds of our designers, instead of in troves of overruns and free-size apparel. Our must-have bags now come from local communities, instead of in iterations of an It bag. Even our chocolate now comes from farms in Davao or Ilocos, instead of a factory-wrapped bar sold in original, jumbo, and fun sizes.

An entrepreneurial spirit has emboldened local tastemakers, many of whom even integrate marginalized sectors of society or ethnic communities in the process. And that success is not unevenly distributed— brands and creatives, young and old alike, whether purporting a traditionally Filipino craft or re-interpreting it into something less straightforward, have created a distinct visual identity unique to these 7,000 or so islands we call home.

—ANDREA ANG

SMALLER
AND
SMALLER
CIRCLES
F.H. BATACAN

MODERN STUFF:

Locals' Own

There are two sides to contemporary Philippine-made goods.

The first are of those beholden to the elements of tropicana. Whether it's hand-dyed swimmers from Eairth (which has made it all the way to Barney's and other international stockists), linen jumpsuits by Aráw, all-natural beauty brand Prim Botanicals, or the vibrant colors of Happy Skin's lipsticks, many of them perpetuate life lived constantly on vacation, which is apt, given the climate.

The other are the progressives who have successfully integrated Philippine culture with an instinct for the current. Long-listed for the LVMH Prize in 2014, exciting young designer Carl Jan Cruz makes unisex denim and raw pieces in step with the global style aesthetic of relaxed authenticity. F.H. Batacan's crime novel *Smaller and Smaller Circles*, which has since been adapted into a film by the director Raya Martin, is set in the harrowingly familiar setting of corrupt Manila. The dynastic accessories brand Aranáz is constantly spotted in the pages of *Elle* and *Harper's Bazaar* for their cheeky use of local materials in hits such as their pineapple bags and pompom earrings. *Vogue* talent Ken Samudio, under his diffusion line Matthew & Melka, draws inspiration from his former occupation as a marine biologist to create pieces such as his clip-on flower earrings, which are handmade by disadvantaged women using indigenous materials. Even brands which tend toward the minimalist—such as "Basics with a twist" purveyors Harlan + Holden and jewelry brand Stocketon Row—all have an inherent cheekiness about them, a playfulness that Filipinos themselves have long since been characterized.

Store Info

CLOCKWISE FROM TOP LEFT

① **Carl Jan Cruz Jeans**
Available at Carl Jan Cruz
45 Bayani Rd, Taguig City
Appointments at
carljancruz.com

② **Aranáz Bag**
Available at Aranáz
Greenbelt 5, Makati

③ **Harlan + Holden Shoes**
Available at Harlan + Holden
PowerPlant Mall, Makati

④ **Stockton Row Bracelets**
Available at Cura V
PowerPlant Mall, Makati

⑤ **Eairth Swimmer**
Available at Tropa
117 Aguirre St., Legazpi
Village, Makati

⑥ **Araw Jumpsuit**
Available at Tropa
117 Aguirre St., Legazpi
Village, Makati

⑦ **Prim Botanicals Face Oil**
Available at Lanai
The Alley at Karrivin Plaza, 2316
Chino Roces Ext., Makati

⑧ **Happy Skin Shut Up & Kiss Me Moisturizing Lippie**
Available at Happy Skin
Glorietta 3, Ayala Center, Makati

Aranáz Earrings
⑨ Available at Aranáz
Greenbelt 5, Makati

⑩ ***Smaller and Smaller Circles* by F.H. Batacan**
Available at National
Bookstore
Stores nationwide

⑪ **Matthew and Melka by Ken Samudio Flower Earrings**
Available at Lanai
The Alley at Karrivin Plaza, 2316
Chino Roces Ave., Makati

T SHIRTS:

The Souvenir Tee

Forget the magnet. Nowadays, the new trophy souvenir is the effortless cool of a t-shirt. As the iconic giant of local retail, it would not be unheard of to guess that there is at least one article of Bench clothing in every Filipino's wardrobe. Less obvious choices are Float, which makes sea-to-shore swimwear meant to accompany weekends in La Union or Baler; and Proudrace, the grunge and '90s-inspired casual fashion brand. Out of all options, however, Team Manila shows the most intimate knowledge of the true Filipino identity, taking slang and experience from the street and into their designs. Still, we are partial to a brightly colored t-shirt screaming "Boracay"—there is, after all, nothing else quite like it.

Store Info

CLOCKWISE FROM TOP LEFT

① **Team Manila T-Shirt**
Available at Market! Market!
McKinley Parkway, Taguig

② **Bench Tank Top**
Available at Bench
stores nationwide

③ **Bench Boxer Shorts**
Available at Bench
stores nationwide

④ **Float Swimwear T-Shirt**
Available at Adora
Greenbelt 5, Ayala Center, Makati

⑤ **Proudrace T-Shirt**
Available at
proudrace.com

INDIGENOUS INSPIRATION:

Aesthetic Immersion

The hands of the Philippines' prized artisans hold some of the country's longest traditions and techniques. As such, some brands have made them their advocacies—social enterprise Anthill uses materials from weaving communities all over the country to create interesting pieces such as cropped ternos, handkerchief skirts, bowties, and tube scarves; while Great Women empowers females from marginalized sectors as they make bold, graphic hand-beaded pieces that their tribes are known for.

There is also a wave of younger brands who are working to create more modernized offerings. Piopio in particular walks that line carefully, using inabel in updated silhouettes for the bohemian at heart. Abacá Store curates pieces made from its namesake, the Philippines' most popular natural material. Meanwhile, Halo + Halo's accessories focuses more on creating pieces that embody Filipino culture, referencing Spanish, American, and Chinese influences to truly represent the so-called melting pot—a little bit of everything, to represent such a distinct people.

Store Info

CLOCKWISE FROM TOP LEFT

① **Piopio Dress**
Available at
piopio.ph

② **Piopio Skirt**
Available at
piopio.ph

③ **Anthill Skirt**
Available at Tesoro's
Antonio Arnaiz Ave., Makati

④ **Great Women Bangles**
Available at Tesoro's
Antonio Arnaiz Ave., Makati

⑤ **Halo + Halo Bag**
Available at
halohalostore.ph

⑥ **Great Women Espadrilles**
Available at Tesoro's
Antonio Arnaiz Ave., Makati

⑦ **Abacá Store Bag**
Available at
abacastore.com

⑧ **Anthill Containers**
Available at Tesoro's
Antonio Arnaiz Ave., Makati

FOOD:

Everyday Fiesta

Store Info

CLOCKWISE FROM TOP LEFT

A remnant of the Spanish colonial era, the fiesta is long-standing tradition in major cities across the Philippines's many islands. Some are religious, some are rituals, some are related to harvest—but all involve merriment and an overflowing buffet table. There is no such thing as a standard menu, but if not for some sort of kakanin (rice cake), there might be corned beef of either the beloved Purefoods or the flavorful Delimondo sort. Sweets will also be in abundance. Try hot chocolate (with ensaymada) from the award-winning Malagos chocolate farm, or the unapologetically hipster bean-to-bar Tigre Y Oliva, or just good old Chocnut.

Drinking is of course heavily involved in the traditions of this beer-drinking country. If it's not a San Miguel Pale Pilsen or homebrewed lambanog, you'll see Don Papa Rum, small-batch rum distilled in the foothills of Mt Kanlaon in Negros, perfect for the discerning gentleman (or woman); or even the calamansi or dalandan flavoured liqueur by the country's oldest distillery, Destileria Limtuaco. Pair it with a sobering cup of coffee from Kalsada's Benguet- and Bukidnon-sourced beans, but if not, a pack of Boy Bawang chichacorn should never be far behind.

① **Don Papa Rum**
Available in groceries nationwide

② **Destileria Limtuaco Manille Liqueur de Calamansi and Dalandan**
Available in groceries and convenience stores nationwide

③ **Delimondo Corned Beef**
Available in groceries and convenience stores nationwide

④ **Purefoods Corned Beef**
Available in groceries and convenience stores nationwide

⑤ **Boy Bawang**
Available in groceries and convenience stores nationwide

⑥ **Kalsada Coffee Pack**
Available at The Den
Hub: Make Lab, First United Building, Escolta St, Manila

⑦ **Tigre y Olivia Chocolate**
Available at Holy Carabao
6241 R Palma St., Makati

⑧ **Abacá Store Mother of Pearl Utensils**
Available at
abacastore.com

⑨ **Malagos Hot Chocolate**
Available at Kultura in SM Supermalls nationwide

⑩ **Kultura Marble Dish**
Available at Kultura in major SM Supermalls

⑪ **Chocnut**
Available in groceries and convenience stores nationwide

GREENHILLS SHOPPING CENTER

TIANGGES AND BAZAARS:

Gold Rush

"Tiangge" is an Aztec term, derived from the language Nahuatl, but it has become so ingrained in Filipino that it's hard to imagine it as anything but. Essentially a flea market maze of crowded stalls with merchandise running from floor to ceiling, tiangges are bargain mecca. These small businesses offer the lowest prices to be had, whether you're angling for dried mangoes or apparel sourced from all over Asia.

Where to Go

Greenhills

The classic and perhaps most reliable option is the Greenhills tiangge. Airconditioned and relatively safe, it's also one of the most organized.

Greenhills Shopping Center
Ortigas Ave., Greenhills, San Juan

Divisoria

The behemoth of all tiangges is Divisoria, deep in Chinatown. Spend the entire day at 168 Shopping Mall and its surrounding area, and come prepared to haggle.

168 Shopping Mall
Recto Ave., Divisoria, Manila

Market! Market!

Market! Market! is a labyrinth, with multiple tiangges happening at any given time throughout its halls, but head outside to the open area for a selection of delicacies from all over the country, arranged by province.

Market! Market!
McKinley Parkway, Taguig

St. Francis Square

St. Francis Square is one of the newer tiangge centers, located right across SM Megamall. It does, however, feature all tiangge classics: taho, fluorescent lights, and a lot of negotiation.

St. Francis Square
Bank Dr., Ortigas Center, Pasig

Short and Sweet

The Philippines has an incredible bespoke fashion industry that will reward those who can't bear to leave paradise. But for those visiting for less than a week, there are plenty of ways to experience Pinoy craftsmanship.

Go Online

Float Swimwear

Float offers chic rashguards and swimwear made for the surfer girl in all of us—with, yes, a plus size range. Don't miss their other beach-to-city essentials, like the "Manila girl" sweaters and hand-painted skate decks. *Available at floatswimwear.com*

Halo + Halo

The family-owned accessories brand executes practical Filipino mainstays like a banig mat, bayong tote, and multi-purpose ottomans using recycled materials and subdued colours. *Available at halohalostore.ph*

Stockton Row

Despite drawing inspiration from international travels, this elegant jewelry brand has a distinctly local vibe thanks to its similarities to the ancient gold jewelry worn by our ancestors. *Available at stocktonrow.com*

Renegade Folk

If you can't make it to shoe capital Marikina, Renegade Folk is the next best thing. The young team works with Marikina's famed sapateros to create contemporary sandals for men, women, and children. *Available at renegadefolk.com*

Rraw

This Iloilo-based skincare brand is 100% plant-powered. Created using only fresh and wild ingredients, RRAW specializes in cleansing bars, scrubs, and sponges that will make any set of cheeks grin. *Available at rraw.ph*

Go Out

Kultura Filipino

Kultura Filipino, a handicraft and lifestyle retail store found in SM malls, is a veritable crash course in Filipino culture. It features pieces from all over the country, showcasing the best of each province—hand-carved wooden items from Baguio, marble homeware from Romblon, lambanog from Quezon—all in one place. *Major SM malls all over the city*

Hub: Make Lab

In an effort to revive Escolta, creatives have come together to bring it back to its former glory under the First United Building roof. From vintage collectors' items to handmade journals, Pinoy-themed perfumes to prepackaged edibles, Escolta has once again become a go-to place for a leisurely weekend. *First United Building, Escolta St. Binondo*

Tropa Store

The outrageously hip Tropa specializes in the laid back lifestyle, stocking a tightly-curated assortment of exclusives from Aráw and Eairth, an in-house unisex line, Ilog Maria bath products, independent publications, and vintage eyewear. *117 Aguirre St. Makati*

Lanai

This multi-brand concept store features homeware, flowers, clothes, and a café. Its second floor features the best of locally made goods, including embroidered shorts by Anne Marie Saguil and rope sandals by Island Girl, that are appropriate for the 24/7 vacation mindset. *The Alley at Karrivin Plaza, 2316 Chino Roces Ext., Makati*

Cura V

Small but stocked to the brim with chic knickknacks, Cura V is a look into jewelry box of Manila's most fashionable. Their most prized pieces include those of Natalya Lagdameo, designer of the incredibly beloved giniling bangles inspired by Ifugao traditions. *Power Plant Mall, Rockwell Center, Makati*

Thank You

This book would not be possible without the help of the following:

Carlos Celdran

Marika Constantino
and Gab Villegas
of 98B Collaboratory

Arts Serrano of One/Zero

The Public School Manila

Gino Chua

Alicia Sy

Trickie Lopa

Mara Coson

Sasha Lim Uy Mariposa

Yvette Fernandez

Daryl Chang

Agoo Bengzon

Bucky's Soft Serve
for being the indulgence
that kept the editors sane

Lisa Gokongwei, Christine Ko,
Lio Mangubat, Mica de Leon, and
the rest of the Summit Books team

Raymond Ang is a writer, editor, publisher, and executive producer. He is a columnist at the *Philippine Star*, a publisher at CNN Philippines, and the editor of several bestselling books. He won a Golden Dove Award for producing the CNN Philippines series *Leading Women* and an Adobo Design Award for editing *Benchmark*, local retail giant Bench's in-store magazine. In 2015, he creative-directed Bench's "Love Local," a campaign championing Philippine pop culture icons Eddie Garcia and Pilita Corrales, as well as "Love All Kinds of Love," a campaign promoting equal love. His writing has appeared in *Rolling Stone Italia, L'Officiel Manila, Esquire Philippines*, and *Rogue Magazine*.

raymondangas

Made of Bricks

Made of Bricks is an editorial imprint founded by Raymond Ang under Summit Publishing Co., Inc. With sharp design, ambitious editorial direction, and a healthy disposition for all things digital, Made of Bricks believes that this Instagram-obsessed, ADD-afflicted generation still has an affinity for books and the printed page provided they're produced in the way they understand them.

The first release under Made of Bricks was the bestseller *Push: Muses, Mischief & How to Make it in Manila* (2015), a book by top young photographer BJ Pascual.

madeofbricksph

SERIOUS STUDIO

Serious Studio creates brand identities, strategies, communications, websites, experiences, and other big words. This bunch believes that effective communication happens when you Make Sense and Look Good™. They work with clients to create authentic and interesting brands for the world.

serious-studio.com seriousstudio

EDITOR
Raymond Ang

CREATIVE DIRECTION
Serious Studio

MANAGING EDITOR
Manica C. Tiglao

FOOD & DINING EDITOR
Michelle V. Ayuyao

ASSISTANT EDITOR
Don Jaucian

STAFF PHOTOGRAPHER
JL Javier

WRITERS
Apa Agbayani, Michi Ancheta, Andrea Ang, Nicole Curato, Arianna Lim,
Paolo Lorenzana, Miguel Ortega, Gabbie Tatad

PHOTOGRAPHERS
Gabby Cantero, Tammy David, Paul Del Rosario, Jojo Gloria, Kai Huang,
Czar Kristoff, Toto Labrador, Miguel Nacianceno, Renzo Navarro, Mark
Nicdao, William Ong, BJ Pascual, Joseph Pascual, Jericho San Miguel, Ian
Santos, Macoy Sison, Sonny Thakur

MADE OF BRICKS is an imprint of Raymond Ang published by
Summit Publishing Co., Inc.
7/F Robinsons Cybergate 3, Pioneer Street, Mandaluyong City, Philippines 1550
www.summitmedia.com.ph

SUMMIT
BOOKS